Living Meditation, Living Insight

The Path of Mindfulness in Daily Life

by
Dr. Thynn Thynn

Dedicated to my teachers and to my family

Dr. San Lin, Win and Tet.

Foreword

I am very impressed by the thoroughness and care with which Dr. Thynn Thynn explains the path of mindfulness in daily life in her book. This has not been emphasized as strongly in the monastic and meditative teachings of Buddhism that have taken root in the West. In fact, much of Buddhist practice in Asia has followed the intensive model. But clearly, that will not work for those of us who are house-holders in the West. And anyway, the wonderful experiences of intensive practice often lead to less transformation of our lives than we might hope, so that after intensive meditation practice we are back again in the midst of our lives with the question of how to bring the Dhamma to bear in everyday life. I am so pleased when I see a book like Dr. Thynn Thynn's that speaks directly to this situation.

I applaud her clarity and courage for teaching in the straightforward way that she does.

Jack Kornfield
Spirit Rock Center
Woodacre, California
July 1992

Introduction

Years ago when I came to Thynn-Thynn's small Dharma group in Bangkok, I was a newcomer to Buddhism. Thynn-Thynn opened the door to her home and welcomed me with warm eyes and an infectious laugh. Several of her friends joined us and began asking her questions about Buddhism. Smiling, she answered them in a casual way, often using personal anecdotes.

As the years went by, the group grew. Friends invited their curious friends to come. Thynn-Thynn responded by offering more structured sessions. We literally sat at her feet as she gave a discourse, drew diagrams, and defined Pali terms. After a lunch filled with laughter and talk, we met again for lively discussions. Someone would ask for clarification of a point. The discussion would roll around to: How can I apply this in my life? How will it help me be mindful around my little toddlers? How can I practice equanimity with my rebellious teenagers? How can I share this with a closed-minded spouse? How can I be more compassionate to a friend in need?

Thynn-Thynn would gently offer, in a soft voice, her insights. Rather than suggest a specific solution, she would propose a Dharma way of looking at a problem. The questioner would return home and try "stopping and looking" and "letting go." That was our practice. Go home and try it out.

Over the years, we became a support group, but one with a difference. The Dharma propelled us forward in our lives; it held us together as a group. It wasn't always easy. We were all so different – or so we thought at first. We came from many countries – Burma, Thailand, Sri Lanka, Mexico, Switzerland, Russia and the United States. We were an eclectic mix of religious backgrounds – Buddhist, Catholic, Protestant, Jewish, Muslim and atheist. And we had very different personalities – devotional, intellectual, artistic, outgoing and contemplative. In a sense, we were speaking different languages: the logic of the intellectual left the devotional unmoved; dramatic insights overwhelmed those with more reserved temperaments. Sometimes sparks would fly at meetings. But Thynn-Thynn leavened these delicate situations with her ready humor and perceptive awareness. The social interactions within the group itself also became part of our practice.

Going one step further, Thynn-Thynn customized the practice for each of us. She matched, point for point, the heated arguments of the intellectual. She urged artists to delight in the beauty of the moment. Nurturing each person's natural tendencies, she encouraged each person to open up and blossom. Acutely sensitive to each person's needs, Thynn-Thynn sought to balance our rigid conditioning. She prodded the lazy, shocked the arrogant, and relaxed the compulsive. In doing so, she revealed many different paths to understanding.

Gradually, each of us softened into Buddhism. We found we smiled more, laughed more and loved more. We slowed down and had glimpses of things as they are.

Recently, Thynn-Thynn has moved to the United States; new friends gather around, eager to learn the Dharma and apply it to their daily lives. The Bangkok group still continues. Those of us who were in the original group remain friends and continue to practice, although we are separated by years and miles. Despite our differences, we found we have a lasting commitment to living the Dharma, and an abiding love for the woman who showed us it can be done.

Pam Taylor

Preface to the Second Edition

Ten years ago, when our small Dhamma group started to meet in Bangkok, I was inspired to write about the many questions that arose. The articles compiled in this book came out of those many discussions. As I wrote, I gave these articles to Dhamma friends to help them digest the Dhammic point of view and encourage them in their spiritual quests.

I wrote the articles to encourage practitioners learning to meditate in daily life. In this sense, the articles are presented as a "hands-on" or, more accurately, a "minds-on" training manual. Although I discuss meditation in general, the real focus is on how the Dhamma brings us into spontaneous, wholesome and creative living.

This book is primarily for beginners in meditation. I have used theory and Pali terms sparingly. The emphasis is on the process and insights into the nature of the mind. My objective in presenting the articles is to help the aspirant build up a solid foundation of mindfulness as a way of life rather than as a practice separated from daily living. For those who have been practicing meditation in the formal way, this approach can help them incorporate their mindfulness practice into everyday experience. The process of mindfulness is the same, except in one important aspect: instead of sitting down, closing the eyes and watching the mind, the practice is done while attending to everyday business.

After the first edition of this book came out in 1992, I received comments to the effect that my teaching style is similar to Krishnamurti and Zen. When someone once mentioned it to my friend, the Theravada nun Shinma Dhammadina, she replied, "That's because her teachers' teachings are very much like Krishnamurti and Zen."

My teachers are Burmese abbots, Sayadaw U Eindasara of Rangoon and Sayadaw U Awthada of Henzada. They are Theravada monks, but teach the Dhamma in a very unorthodox and dynamic fashion. They veer away from the emphasis on the traditional form of "sitting" meditation, and instead strongly emphasize "looking directly within and practicing mindfulness in everyday life."

I was very much attracted to this approach because of its simplicity, directness and practicality in daily life. Just before I met my teachers in 1973, I had meditated briefly in the traditional sitting style at the Mahasi Meditation Center in Rangoon with the late Sayadaw U Zawana. After a few sessions with him, I began to realize I was automatically becoming aware of my feelings in daily life and was becoming much calmer without formal "sitting in meditation." I discovered that as soon as I focused on my feelings they would drop away very quickly. Then, through some good Dhamma friends, I found out about my teachers' method of finding peace of mind by stopping and looking at the mind, moment by moment, in daily life as a form of meditation practice. I felt immediately drawn to this style of teaching since I was experiencing exactly what these teachers taught.

When I met my teachers, I was struck by the Sayadaws' profound wisdom and their innovative style of teaching. Their liberal interpretation of Theravada Buddhism is rarely found in traditional Buddhist Myanmar. Their teachings may sound similar to Krishnamurti's, in an attempt to break down the mind from all conditioning to its ultimate freedom, but what is striking in the approach of the Sayadaws is that they provide a means to reassimilate the relative with a new insightful perspective. They are also exceptionally skillful in providing hands-on training which is similar to a direct transmission in the Zen tradition. This is probably why my book may appear to some as an integration of Theravada Buddhism, Krishnamurti and Zen. My teachers have not been Western-educated, and came to know about Krishnamurti and Zen only when we, their students, introduced them to these teachings. It is thus interesting to see the confluence of such apparently disparate approaches to spiritual truth in such an unlikely manner.

I am often asked what my teachers were like. They are actually an unlikely pair. Sayadaw U Eindasara is a profound mystic and poet and the quieter one of the pair. We fondly call him "the laughing Buddha." He rarely appears or talks in public but devotes extraordinary energy to working with his students. Sayadaw U Awthada is brilliant and quick-witted and we called him "the Burmese Zen Master" in recognition of his Zen-like ability to tie up his students in knots and push them beyond the intellect.

These teachers invite comparisons with Krishnamurti in that they live a very simple life, without seeking followers, without setting up any institutions or organizations, and keeping away from publicity and fame. They still live and teach within the confines of monkhood, yet maintain an integrity and openness rarely found in Buddhist Asia.

I had the good fortune to study closely with these two remarkable teachers and I remember with fondness and gratitude the time I spent training with them. They thought I was a little tricky, as I would continuously bring people from all walks of life to be exposed to their teaching firsthand. From such close encounters I have the privilege now to share my experiences with members of my Dhamma groups and also, through this book, with many others. To these two teachers, I bow in great reverence; I also bow down to my guru, Shwe Baw Byun Sayadaw, for his kind support for this book and for my Dhamma work in the West.

Thynn Thynn
Scarsdale, New York, 1995

9

Acknowledgements

I am deeply indebted to my dearest Dhamma friend, Pam Taylor, who was the very first person to suggest that I should get my writings published, and who also took it upon herself to better organize my random writing and restructure it into a manuscript. Without her valiant efforts and superb editing, my manuscript would still be lying on a shelf in my basement. My thanks also go to Marcia Hamilton, who edited the first draft manuscript, and to Ashin U Tay Zaw Batha, who edited the text. Then it was my illustrious husband, Dr. San Lin, who succeeded in nudging me to complete the manuscript and who was enormously helpful in preparing the final version.

It is not only to my husband, but to my wonderful children, Win and Tet, that I owe many insights into myself, human nature and family life. Many friends ask me what my meditation is and I always reply, "My family is my meditation." It is mostly through my family that I have learned to practice what I preach. It is the family that compels me to sharpen my wits, to train and retrain my own mindfulness. In fact, my family is my greatest challenge and training ground.

I am very grateful to my old Dhamma friends from Bangkok for the memorable and joyous times I had with them and for their candid and challenging questions which resulted in this book.

My deep appreciation goes also to Jane Hein of Scarsdale, N.Y. and Dagmar Annabelle Zinser of Germany for their generous donations in funding this entire second edition. Thanks also to Dr. Hla Myint and Becky Myint from Australia for their kind contribution and to the many others who have contributed over time.

Many thanks to John Hein and Charlotte Richardson for their careful editing and revising, to Nee Nee Myint for retyping, and to David Babski for formatting the manuscript.

Lastly, I would like to thank the The Corporate Body of the Buddha Educational Foundation, of Taipei, Taiwan for publishing this edition, and Mr. Tsu-Ku Lee of Chuang Yen Temple, Carmel, New York, for making this possible.

Thynn Thynn

Contents

The Path of Sukkhavipassaka

Samatha *practices such as* anapanasati *meditations on the breath are not particularly necessary on the Path of Sukkhavipassaka. Together with observance of the three* sila *(moral precepts),* pañña *(wisdom) can be developed. When the two* pañña *factors develop, the three* samadhi *factors are also developed concomitantly. This is known as* pañcangika magga. *Herein Five Path factors are together integratedly developed. In conjunction with the three* sila *factors, they make up the Noble Eightfold Path.*

Practicing this Path will also relieve mental afflictions. To practice this path requires a high level of intelligence, effort and perseverance.

Ledi Sayadaw
(Magganga Dipani)

FREEDOM TO BEGIN

What is it to be free?

IN THE BUDDHIST SENSE, "free" means to be free from all suffering, to reach inner freedom where suffering ceases to be. This is, of course, an ideal state of mind – but how do we reach it? To reach inner freedom we must search for freedom with a "free mind." It is like the saying, "to catch a thief one must think like a thief." The sort of freedom one is trying to find is an absolute state – nothing less – infinite, unbounded and limitless. We are starting out with a mind that is finite, intellect-bound and already limited in itself. If we crowd this with all sorts of ideals, concepts, doctrines and judgments, the mind – which is already weighed down by its own burden – can never be free enough to experience truth in its entirety. It can only accept the truth or experience within the limits of doctrines, beliefs and concepts, which are products of the intellect. The mind can never break out of the intellectual conditioning we are trying to transcend. By clinging to a specific system or format in the search for inner freedom, we will be able to experience only that which the system or format allows. But Truth is infinite, unpossessed, unbounded. It does not belong to any religion, sect or system. All religions, all methods, all systems improvised by humankind are attempts to guide us on the path to Truth. Often, though, the "way" is mistaken for the "Truth."

The mind in search of its own freedom must first of all assume an impersonal attitude, which leaves it free to explore, investigate, examine and, most important of all, to "experience." Most of us start with a personal need to find an inner freedom. In this state it is rather difficult to assume an impersonal approach, but such is the paradox of the inner path. As soon as we become personal, we tend to be judgmental and opinionated. Judgments and discriminations arise out of an intellectual and conditioned mind. As soon as one makes a judgment and discriminates, the intellect is at work. So long as the intellect is at the forefront of one's mind, it will always obstruct one's ability to experience fully one's own inner depth and essence. This is the reason that all the ways and means to liberation – the inner paths – transcend the intellect and move into the realm of the intuitive or the spiritual, for only the intuitive aspect of our mind can experience and realize Truth or freedom in its entirety. Different religious systems have developed methods and styles particular to their own historical, cultural and emotional backgrounds. Each of us is left to find the right path for ourselves.

Whichever path one may adopt, the greatest danger is the accumulation of emotional possessions. These are "my" guru, "my" beliefs, "my" progress, "my" experience. Here again, one faces a paradox. A teacher's guidance is invariably necessary for one to proceed properly on the path, but it presents a hindrance if one is not careful. The most common problem is personally clinging to gurus and teachers. In fact, this is one of the most difficult hindrances to overcome in all quests for inner freedom. Letting go of beliefs, doctrines, gurus, ideals and judgments is extremely difficult, because one holds them very dear to oneself. They become one's possessions, like material wealth and power, and then one is not free and does not proceed further.

So what should one do? The only appropriate way is to view everything with equanimity, be it gurus, doctrines, ideals, and even one's own practice and progress. Only then can one view everything with objectivity.

Freedom is not just an end result. It is not something that awaits us at the end of our endeavor. Freedom is instantaneous, right now, from the very beginning. We can be "free" in the very process of the search, in experiencing, in every step along the way.

To achieve freedom requires only two things:
a silent mind and an open heart.

Living Meditation

It is not entirely necessary that in vipassana *practice*
one achieve a tranquil state through samatha *practices.*
What is crucial is pañña paramita *in the individual
(the inherent quality of intelligence). If a person has the
necessary* pañña paramita *and is ready for it, he or she
can attain enlightenment even by just listening to a
discourse. Hence, based on a person's* pañña paramita,
*enlightenment can be achieved while living a household
life and contemplating* anicca *(impermanence) within
or without his or her own self, within or without his
or her own home life.*

Ledi Sayadaw
(Vipassana Dipani)

A: I have a lot of worries and stress. I try to meditate in order to relax, but it is no use.

T: In this fast-moving world, meditation is regarded as an instant remedy for life's ills. If you look upon meditation as merely a tranquilizer, you are underestimating its true value. Yes, relaxation does occur through meditation, but that is only one of its many results. Meditation in Buddhism is neither an instant cure nor just a stress-relieving measure.

Meditation in Buddhism means cultivation of the mind in order to achieve insight wisdom or *pañña*, ultimately leading to liberation or *nibbana*.

D: Nibbana aside, I want to meditate, but I cannot find the time.

When you speak of meditation, you may think of the type of meditation that is popular these days, the sitting form of meditation. But that form is merely an aid, a support to develop a mental discipline of mindfulness and equanimity. The form should not be mistaken for the path.

The popular notion is that you need to set aside a special time or place to meditate. In actuality, if meditation is to help you acquire peace of mind as you function in your life, then it must be a dynamic activity, part and parcel of your daily experience. Meditation is here and now, moment-to-moment, amid the ups and downs of life, amid conflicts, disappointments and heartaches – amid success and stress. If you want to understand and resolve anger, desires, attachments and all the myriad emotions and conflicts, need you go somewhere else to find the solution? If your house was on fire, you wouldn't go somewhere else to put out the fire, would you?

If you really want to understand your mind, you must watch it while it is angry, while it desires, while it is in conflict. You must pay attention to the mind as the one-thousand-and-one thoughts and emotions rise and fall. The moment you pay attention to your emotions, you will find that they lose their strength and eventually die out. However, when you are inattentive, you find that these emotions go on and on. Only after the anger has subsided are you aware that you have been angry. By then, either you have made some unwanted mistakes or you have ended up emotionally drained.

R: How do you handle these emotions? I know that when I am angry I want to shout and throw things. Should I control these emotions or express them?

The natural inclination is to try to control the emotions. But when they are kept under a lid, they try to escape. They either rush out with a bang or they leak out as sickness or neuroses.

R: What should I do? Do I let my emotions go wild?

Certainly not. That is exactly what we don't want to do. That is another extreme – to release your emotions impulsively. The important thing is neither control nor non-control. In either situation you are working up your desire to control. Neither situation is tenable. So long as this desire occupies your mind, your mind is not free to see anger as it is. Hence another paradox arises: the more you want to be free of the anger, the more you are not free of it.

To understand the mind, you have to watch and pay attention with an uncluttered, silent mind. When your mind is chattering away, all the time asking questions, then it lacks the capacity to look. It is too busy asking questions, answering, asking.

Try to experience watching yourself in silence. That silence is the silence of the mind free from discriminations, free from likes and dislikes, free from clinging.

Thoughts and emotions by themselves are just momentary and possess no life of their own. By clinging to them, you prolong their stay.

Only when your mind is free from clinging and rejecting can it see anger as anger, desire as desire. As soon as you
"see," your mental process is fully preoccupied with "seeing," and in that split second anger dies a natural death. This
seeing, or insight, called *pañña*, arises as a spontaneous
awareness that can be neither practiced nor trained. This
awareness brings new insight into life, new clarity and new
spontaneity in action.

So, you see, meditation need not be separate from life
and its daily ups and downs. If you are to experience peace
in this everyday world, you need to watch, understand and
deal with your anger, desire and ignorance as they occur.
Only when you cease to be involved with your emotions
can the peaceful nature of your mind emerge. This peace-
nature enables you to live every moment of your life completely. With this newfound understanding and awareness,
you can live as a complete individual with greater sensitivity. You will come to view life with new and fresh perceptions. Strangely enough, what you saw as problems before
are problems no more.

Staying with the Moment

R: You say I can meditate in daily life by cultivating sati *(paying attention) in my mind. But I find that very difficult; my mind is too distracted.*

T: That is not unusual. You see, to focus on your mind as you function in everyday life, you need to turn your mind inside out. Indeed, your mind must be strong and focused in order to be mindful of itself. So naturally it is difficult to focus on your mind if you are agitated or distracted.

R: How can I start then?

Try being mindful of whatever you are doing at the moment – walking, sitting, bathing, cleaning, looking at a flower. You can do this at any time and in any place. As you train your mind to focus, you will find you are less distracted. Later, as you go on, you can be mindful of your thoughts and emotions as they arise.

Suppose you are driving. You have to pay attention to the driving, don't you? Your mind has to be there at the time and place of driving, concentrating on the road, watching the other drivers. You cannot afford to be distracted too much by other thoughts. It is something like meditation on the task at hand. But often we do not carry out other tasks in this concentrated way.

D: Why not?

Probably because they are less dangerous than driving. But you can apply the same principle to other activities. Suppose you are eating. If your mind is distracted, you may not even be aware of tasting the food, let alone enjoying it. Only when you focus on eating can you really enjoy the food.

The same is true even in passive activities. Suppose you are sitting on a bus. Try simply to be where you are, rather than letting your mind wander. Train your mind to focus on your surroundings. Be aware of the other people on the bus, how fast the bus is going, and where it is going. This is a very good way to start meditation. Simply be where you are rather than letting your mind roam.

P: I have tried being mindful of the moment. But it is strenuous and I get all tangled up.

For goodness sakes, staying with the moment is only a figure of speech. It is not a commandment to be followed rigidly. This is not a proficiency test. You must understand this from the outset; otherwise you will be tied up in knots trying too hard every second of the day.

If you become too involved with staying in the moment, you lose the art of living – of free flowing.

You must realize that staying with the moment is just a means to break the mind's old habits. Usually the mind flitters between thoughts and feelings about the past, present and future. Staying with the moment is just a way to train the mind to cease flitting.

It is not important that you be with the moment every single moment of the day. What is important is that you learn to get out of the constant mental run-around and to be more focused and grounded.

Once you break the habit of the roaming mind, you will find you are more centered and more with the present moment.

SD: What do we gain from this?

That is a very pertinent question. Of course, you will have better concentration, but you can achieve concentration without learning the art of meditation. Many activities – golf, chess, reading – enhance concentration.

SD: What is the difference between those activities and moment-to-moment meditation?

If you look into the process involved in those activities, you will see an element of desire – the desire to achieve perfection, to win a game, to feel good, whatever. You are motivated by desire. Also, there is an end to the activity and so to the concentration. Concentration is also very important in meditation, but it is not everything. If we simply con n-trate, we will not get any further benefit.

To meditate, it is crucial to be mindful without desire, without aversion, without likes and dislikes, and without goals.

If you can be mindful without judgments and without likes and dislikes, then you are practicing with an inner silence or equanimity, called *upekkha* in Pali.

This is true in both formal sitting meditation and in the informal, unstructured meditation we are discussing now. Two elements are involved: staying with the moment and viewing everything without likes and dislikes.

R: Oh, it's not that easy. We have to do more than just notice our surroundings.

No, it's not easy. That's why it's better to start slowly by focusing on a particular moment. You may not be good at it all at once. But you will find that this practice of staying with the moment facilitates the inner silence. If you concentrate on the moment, and if your concentration is good, then no stray thoughts will enter your mind. As you practice, not only will you be more focused, but you will also become more alert and sensitive to what is happening around you. When your mindfulness is strong, then you can direct your attention inward to your mind, your emotions or your thoughts.

SD: So just being mindful is not enough?

That's right. Being mindful is not sufficient. It is only a means. What is crucial is incorporating equanimity or *upekkha* into your mindfulness.

SD: Will upekkha *lead to inner silence?*

Yes, the only way that will lead the mind to silence is *upekkha*. *Upekkha* is not just a product of meditation training. It is itself a tool in meditation. When you become proficient at looking with equanimity at your own mind, your thoughts and your emotions, then this *upekkha* approach will also spill over into other areas of life. You will begin to listen, look, feel and relate to everything with *upekkha*.

Just mindfulness and concentration do not constitute meditation; equanimity must be a constant ingredient.

SD: Doesn't upekkha *mean detachment?*

Sometimes it is translated as detachment, but that translation is very inadequate. You have to understand that *upekkha* transcends both detachment and attachment. When you are detached, you may also become indifferent if you are not careful. This indifference can lead to dissociation and subtle rejection. *Upekkha* transcends not only non-attachment, but also rejection. The mind is very tricky and has many nuances you have to be aware of.

The full essence of *upekkha* is to go beyond attachment and detachment, beyond likes and dislikes, to relate to things as they are.

So it is crucial that you begin your mindfulness right from the start on the basis of *upekkha*, the nondualistic, the Middle Way. When you can view the world and your own mind or yourself with *upekkha*, then you are already on the right path of meditation.

STAYING WITH MORE MOMENTS

P: Sometimes it's a luxury to be mindful of a task with undivided attention. I only get frustrated if I try to be mindful of a task when my young children demand my attention. It seems like the only thing to do is to redirect my attention to the children and do the task on automatic pilot.

T: I like your phrase "automatic pilot"! Again, I have to emphasize that being mindful is only a means to practice focusing. Don't compete with yourself. What you choose to pay attention to is entirely circumstantial. If the children need you, focus on them.

The only guideline is to avoid rigid conditioning.

This does not mean that if you are cooking vegetables, you must be absolutely mindful of the color and smell of the vegetables and ignore the children's questions. If you did that, you'd be clinging to the cooking.

P: Oh, so that's why I feel frustration?

Yes, because you are clinging. Once again, you must understand that *upekkha* should be in every act. If you can view cooking with *upekkha*, then you won't have a problem letting go of mindfulness on the cooking and you can redirect your attention to the child. Sometimes you can cook – on automatic pilot, as you say – and answer the child. Other times, if the child has a pressing need, you might find it better to stop cooking and really devote all your attention to the child. There are no set rules.

**You can become attached to your mindfulness
of the moment just as you can become
attached to anything else.**

This is very subtle, but understand from the outset that

23

you can be bound by your own mindfulness!

P: If things are very hectic I cannot even redirect my attention to another activity, but find I have to just live in the chaos.

Well, letting go of the mindfulness can be appropriate. But we must also talk about living in the chaos. How do you deal with the chaos?

P: Sometimes I become involved in the chaos and get carried away by it.

Yes, if your mindfulness is not strong enough you can easily be drawn into the chaos. The mindfulness I am talking about is the mindfulness of your own mind. If you are not aware of your thoughts and your feelings about the chaos, you can easily slip into interacting in the situation, reacting to the chaos. Before you know what's happening, you are already storming through the chaos, thus creating more chaos.

If you are mindful of your own feelings as you notice the chaos, you can choose how to act in the situation.

Instead of being only aware of the outside chaos, stop and look directly into yourself and see what is there.

D: But that's not easy.

Of course not. But you have to start somewhere. As long as you are not silent inside, you will always be on a roller coaster ride with the outside chaos.

To look into yourself directly is to come back to your own source and to reach an inner equilibrium and silence. It is only from this inner equilibrium that you can view the outer chaos objectively.

When this happens you can see the chaos as chaos, as only a circumstantial situation. You'll see the cause behind the chaos and you can act accordingly. In short, when you penetrate to the heart of the chaos, you will spontaneously resolve it in the best way for the circumstances. This is what is called penetrating insight wisdom, or *pañña*.

P: Do you mean we should be passive in a chaotic conflict?

No. Again, there is nothing rigid about it. One situation may require a firm hand that cuts right through to the heart of the matter. If you are acting with awareness it will be the right action. Another situation might require that you become quiet and not generate more confusion. If you stop and look, you will know what to do in each situation. If you view both the chaos and your mind with *upekkha*, you will know what to do and will not be bothered by the chaos.

P: If we stop to look, how can we react to others in the right way? We wouldn't have time to think of what to do.

This is the most difficult part to explain. We are so used to functioning with the intellect that it seems quite impossible to function in any given situation without conceptualizing. You see, here we are talking about insight or *pañña*. It's a paradox: insight does not arise unless the conceptualizing stops altogether. In a chaotic situation insight can arise only when we stop conceptualizing about the chaos. Mindfulness of our own mind will in fact stop the conceptualizing that our minds normally go through. When the mindfulness is strong enough and there is total silence in the mind, then insight will spontaneously arise as to how best to deal with the situation at hand.

D: I have another question. I find I can stop being emotional, right in the middle of a difficult interaction, but then I don't know where to go from there. Since I am studying Buddhism and learning to practice the Buddhist way, I feel I should react with more compassion. But I may not feel compassionate. Because I don't know how to go on, I go back to my old conditioning of either resentment or aggressiveness.

My dear, this is only a phase in your own progress. You have come this far. It is possible to go further. Look into the process involved in your mind right in the midst of reacting. When you are able to stop in your tracks, you are already doing quite well.

It is only when you start intellectualizing again that you get into trouble. If you have the notion that as a practicing Buddhist you should be compassionate, then you are setting up an image of yourself. As soon as that thought is allowed to come into your mind, you are not free. At that moment your mind is filled with the desire to fulfill your own image as a practicing Buddhist.

**When the mind is not free, there is no chance
for true compassion to arise.**

It is as simple as that. Only when you free yourself of preconceived perceptions of yourself can spontaneous compassion arise. When you are free of concepts, you will act spontaneously and compassionately as well as creatively.

MEDITATION IN ACTION

D: You say we can work on meditation in our everyday lives. What is the best way to start?

T: Generally speaking, your mind is caught up with the external world and you react to the world in an automatic and habitual manner. When you are preoccupied with the external world, you grossly neglect your mind. The most crucial thing is to realize that you have to redirect this external focus of attention inward, toward your own mind. In other words, learn to be attentive to your mind in the context of daily living – as you eat, work, tend the children, cook, clean, whatever.

R: Do you mean I have to take note of everything that comes into my mind? That would be incredibly difficult. Suppose I'm driving. How can I notice my mind and still pay attention to the road?

That's a very relevant question. It's impossible to take note of your mind all of the time. You would tie yourself up in knots and run off the road. Instead of going to an extreme, begin by concentrating on one particular emotion in yourself. Choose the emotion that bothers you the most, or the one that is most prominent in you. For example, if you tend to be a temperamental kind of person, start by watching your anger. If you are easily hurt, then work with your mood swings. Pay attention to whichever emotion is most noticeable and troublesome to you.

For many people, anger is a good starting point because it is easily noticed and dissolves faster than most other emotions. Once you begin to watch your anger, you will make an interesting discovery. You will find that as soon as you know you are angry, your anger will melt away by itself. It is very important that you watch without likes or dislikes. The more you are able to look at your own anger without making judgments, without being critical, the more easily the anger will dissipate.

27

You may find in the beginning that you notice your anger only when it is about to end. That is not important. The important thing is to decide that you want to focus on your anger. Gradually the watching will become more and more natural. Before long you will notice, suddenly, in the midst of a fit of anger, that your anger drops away without warning. You will find yourself just being aware and no longer entangled in the anger.

A: Can that really happen?

Of course. You see, when you make an effort to turn your attention inward, you are reconditioning yourself. Before this, you were only looking outward. Now you are conditioning yourself anew to look inward some of the time. This looking inward can become habitual; it becomes a kind of conditioning in which your mind automatically focuses on itself at all times. In the beginning this may not be frequent, but don't be discouraged. As time goes on, you will be surprised to find you are aware of your anger sooner than before.

This awareness, when it becomes stronger, will spill over to other emotions. You might find yourself watching your desire. In that watching, the desire will resolve and you will be left only with the awareness. Or you may watch sadness. Sadness is slower to arise and resolve than some other emotions. The most difficult emotion to watch is depression. But that too can be done with stronger mindfulness.

As you get into the swing of it, you will find your awareness becoming sharper. At the same time, the episodes of anger will get shorter and less frequent. As the intensity of anger lessens, you will find you are grappling less and less with your emotions. In the end, you will be surprised to find that you can be friends with your emotions as never before.

R: What do you mean? I can't imagine ever being comfortable with anger.

Because you are no longer struggling with your emotions, you can learn to look at them without judging, clinging or rejecting them. They are no longer threatening to you. You learn to relate to your emotions more naturally, like a witness. Even when you are faced with conflicts and filled with emotions, you can be equanimous with them. As you become more stable, you can deal with conflicts without losing your emotional balance.

D: If my awareness becomes more and more sensitive, is it possible for my mind to know anger as soon as it arises?

Certainly. You see, as your mindfulness becomes stronger and more alert, your mind becomes more aware of its own workings. When mindfulness is complete and dynamic, then you know anger as soon as it arises; as soon as you know it, it begins to dissolve.

D: I have tried watching my anger and I can even see it die down for a moment, but it comes back again and again. Why?

In the initial stages, when mindfulness is still weak and incomplete, anger may die for a moment as you watch. Then, the mind may revert back to its old, habitual angry state. The old conditioning is still strong and you have yet to master the art of mindfulness. You are so used to intellectualizing about the cause of anger – who's to blame, why the conflict escalated, and so on. In fact, this is the mind going back to its treadmill of reacting in the old ways.

You yourself restart the old cycle of creating the anger, thinking about the anger, reacting according to the anger. Here you have anger-intellectualizing-reacting in a vicious cycle.

The purpose of learning to pay attention to anger with a silent mind is to break this cycle of anger and the intellectualization on anger.

The only logical solution is to stop intellectualizing the conflict and simply watch your own mind in the midst of confusion.

R: Do you mean I should just stop thinking in such a situation and do nothing but watch my mind?

That's exactly what I mean.

SD: Suppose I find it difficult to focus on anger. What should I do?

If that is the case, then focus on milder emotions like aversion and desiring. The same thing will happen when you do that. As soon as you are aware of aversion, you will find its intensity decreases; and when your mindfulness becomes strong, the aversion or desiring will resolve. As you proceed and build up your mindfulness, you will find you are able to go on to stronger emotions like anger, craving and greed.

SD: What about problem solving? How can I work my way through complicated situations in which anger and judgment interfere with mindfulness?

It is the same in complicated situations. Let's be very clear – be mindful and watch without judgment. The mindfulness itself trains one towards a pure and simple mind, devoid of judgment and discrimination. To be mindful is a transcending act – transcending anger, transcending judgment. So, if you master the art of mindfulness, you will no longer react with anger or judgment, because paying attention is itself a transcending act.

M: What about other people? How can I react to others? I still need to react to get out of a conflict situation.

That is exactly the point. Most often you are just reacting rather than acting. You are reacting in the ways you have been conditioned. The way to stop reacting is to break that conditioning.

**Stop rationalizing. Stop the thinking mind and
train it to experience itself by watching itself.**

When the mind stops its roller-coaster thinking, it sees
the entire situation as it is. This is crucial. The seeing, the
awareness, is total.

You have to start with yourself. Make the decision to
watch the mind and then see the process. Although you
start with yourself, the actual seeing encompasses the total
situation. You stop seeing yourself in isolation and see yourself instead in the context of the whole situation.

**Then, there is no longer an outside or inside.
You are part of the whole. "You" now, are
not as important as "you" used to be.**

Before, you saw your situation and your own impor-
tance and you needed to guard your identity, to control the
situation. Now, when you see no division between yourself
and others, when you are no more or no less important than
others, only now are you able to grasp the whole situation,
as it is, with clarity. Now you see very clearly where the
problem lies, and instead of reacting, you simply act.

D: Can you give us an example from everyday life?

Would one of you like to give an example?

*P: Let's say my young child is crying because I won't allow him to
have something he wants. If I stop to look, I see my own annoyance
and frustration. I even feel anger, because I cannot reason with the
child. The moment I see that anger, it dissolves – and rather than
responding to my son in anger, I am able to be understanding, yet
firm, towards him. It's strange, because suddenly I know how to
deal with the problem. I don't get involved in his anger and frustrations, or my own. He seems to pick up on this and he becomes
calmer too.*

Yes, that's it. At that moment of seeing your anger, you transcend your own feelings of anger and frustration. You become centered. You no longer generate conflict, and because you are calmer, naturally the child responds.

More often than not, your actions are so complete that the conflict will not continue; you no longer generate reasons for continuing the conflict. This complete, non-generating action in Buddhism is called right action, or *samma kammanta* in Pali. This right action is what I mean by meditation in action. By so doing, you are already on the Noble Eightfold Path.

LETTING GO AND PICKING UP

J: Why is "letting go" so important in Buddhism?

T: The term "letting go" has become a catchword in Buddhist circles. It is true that "letting go" is crucial for arriving at self-realization of inner freedom, but you have to understand how to let go.

J: What are we supposed to let go of?

Let go of your clinging. Let go of the motivating desire behind whatever you're doing. It may be a desire to succeed, to be perfect, to control others or to glorify yourself. It doesn't matter what it is specifically; what matters is the desire behind your act. It is easy to mistake the act for the desire.

**To let go is to let go of clinging to desire,
not to let go of the act.**

We have been talking about stopping and looking at emotions. Try to stop and look at an act; see if you can identify the desire propelling it. When you see the desire, you can also detect the clinging to the desire. When you see the clinging, you see it resolve and you spontaneously let go.

R: There are so many things in life I don't want to renounce or let go of.

Of course not. We don't let go for the sake of letting go. There is a parable about a Zen master who was approached by a pupil. The pupil asked, "I have nothing in my mind now; what shall I do next?" "Pick it up," replied the master. This is an excellent example of the negation that comes with proper understanding, as opposed to pure nihilism.

If we are bound to the concept of letting go, then we are not free. When we are not free, understanding – *pañña* – does not arise. But if we truly see the clinging to desire and let go of it, our act becomes a pure act, without any attendant tensions or frustrations. When the act is pure and simple, we can accomplish more with less stress. At that point, you are "picking up" just as you are "letting go."

D: Why is letting go so difficult? I can watch my other emotions like anger and hatred, but it is much harder to see desire and clinging.

That's because desire and clinging precede anger and hatred. In any fit of emotion – and our mental formations occur so very fast – we can only identify gross emotions like anger and hatred. Desire and clinging are much more subtle, so it takes stronger *samadhi* to be able to see them.

You have been conditioned since you were very young to relate everything to yourself. As soon as you learn to recognize people and things, you're taught how to relate these to the "I" and "mine" – my mom, my dad, my toy, etc. As you grow up you're taught how to relate ideas and concepts to yourself. You have to learn that so that you can function properly in society.

But at the same time, this process slowly and unconsciously creates a concept of selfhood, and you build up your ego. This buildup is strengthened by the values of society. You learn to compete, to achieve, to accumulate knowledge, wealth and power. In other words, you are trained to possess and to cling.

By the time you are grown up, the concept of ego-self has become so real that it is difficult to tell what is illusion and what is reality. It is difficult to realize that "I" and "mine" are temporary, relative and changeable. The same is true of all that is related to "I" and "mine." Not understanding that "I" and "mine" are temporary, you struggle to keep them permanent; you cling to them. This desire to try to keep everything permanent is what makes it so difficult to learn to let go.

M: I have trouble accepting the Buddhist idea of self as an illusion.

You have become so used to functioning with the "I"

and "mine," so used to thinking your "self" is real, that it is naturally difficult to understand the Buddhist way of thinking. The "I" and "mine," being illusions themselves, survive only by clinging to illusions of their own making. They cling to all kinds of mental possessions – be they power, wealth, status or whatever – which are themselves conceptual creations of the mind with no substantial reality. In short, they are also illusions.

R: If "I" is an illusion and not reality, how can "I" get rid of the "I"?

How can you get rid of something that never was?

M: I feel that if I let go of "I" and "mine," I would lose my identity. How can I exist if I let go of everything? Won't I become cold and unfeeling? It sounds scary, like living in a vacuum.

You have to understand that what you lose is merely an illusion. It never was. You empty the mind of illusion about self. Just let go of the illusion.

In fact, you are not losing anything. You just remove an imaginary screen before your eyes. In the process you gain wisdom, or *pañña*. From this wisdom unfold the four virtues of unconditional love, compassion, sympathetic joy and equanimity. These virtues manifest themselves as concern, humanness and sensitivity to others. When you have *pañña* you can fully experience the beauty and warmth that is within all human relationships.

That is why letting go is not losing your illusory ego. You are actually uncovering a great treasure.

PEACE-MIND

IF YOU JUST STOPPED THINKING for a while and sat back to reflect on your own mind, you would be surprised to realize that you are at peace. Even if you agree with me, you might argue that this peace is only temporary. So be it. But let us look into this peaceful tranquil state, temporary or otherwise, since it is already with us – without our having to make any effort at all at being peaceful.

You were born with this peace-nature of the mind; otherwise you would not be what you are, would you? You did not run around meditating to bring about this peace to yourself: you did not learn from someone or some book to make possible this peaceful state in yourself. In other words, "you" had nothing to do with it. Peace is a natural mind-state in every one of us. Peace has been there since the day we were born and it is going to be there till the day we die. It is our greatest gift; so why do we think we have no peace of mind?

Experiencing peace is like looking at our hands. Usually, we see only the fingers – not the spaces in between. In a similar manner, when we look at the mind, we are aware of the active states, such as our running thoughts and the one-thousand-and-one feelings that are associated with them, but we tend to overlook the intervals of peace between them. If one were to be unhappy or sad every minute of the twenty-four-hour day, what would happen to us? I guess we would all be in the mad house!

Then why is it that we supposedly never are at peace?

It is simply because we never allow ourselves to be so.

We enjoy battling with ourselves and our emotions so much that the battle becomes second nature to us. And we complain that we have no peace of mind.

Why don't we leave aside all these complicated ideas for a while and simply contemplate this peaceful nature of ours – since we are fortunate enough to have it – instead of frantically trying to find peace of mind someplace else? How can we find something elsewhere, when it is already in ourselves? Probably that is the reason why we often do not find it.

We do not have to do anything to have this peace, do we? Mind is by itself peaceful.

But we do need to do something to our minds in order to be angry or sad.

Imagine yourself enjoying a moment of quiet. Suddenly something disturbs your enjoyment. You start up at once, annoyed or angry at the disturbance. Why? Because you dislike the interruption. Your mind "acts." It dislikes. It sets up thoughts of dislike, followed by annoyance, anger and a whole series of reactions.

Thought moments are extremely fast, so you don't notice the moment of the mind setting up thoughts of dislike. We generally think that the outside situation is what is responsible for our annoyance. But even during the most durable and miserable experiences of our lives, we find moments when our minds are distracted from the cause of misery and we are relatively free from the devastating emotional state. Once we set our minds back on the event, the unpleasant feelings come rushing in again immediately. When these emotions subside, what happens to them? We seem to take it for granted that they end up or phase out somewhere outside of us. But if they had their origin in the mind, they must surely end in the mind. If they had their origin in a peaceful state, then they would surely end in that peaceful state also. It is only logical.

Let us contemplate this peaceful state. We recognize it before emotions have set in and also after they have disappeared. What about the in-between times? Is peace destroyed during the time that we have been angry or sad? We are so used to implying that this or that destroys our peace of mind that we have come to assume that peace of mind is a contrived state that can be arrived at or deleted at will.

But this is not the case. Peace and tranquillity are part and parcel of our own mental makeup. If they are destroyed during emotional upheavals, our minds might as well be destroyed too. Peace is the essence of our own innate nature and can never be destroyed.

Peace is with us every single moment of our life, but we do not recognize it. This is because we are ignorant about peace – most of the time we are too preoccupied with the external world and our own running thoughts and emotions to be aware of it. We have lost touch with our inner selves, with what is the best in us. We frantically try to find the answer outside when all the time peace is sitting there, silently waiting until we come home to it.

NON-PEACE

IF WE AGREE that have innate peace, what do you think gives us non-peace? From the standpoint of peace of mind, thoughts by themselves are neither good nor bad. It is only when the concepts of "I" and "mine" arise that the mind is thrown into conflict. Likes and dislikes quickly follow these concepts of self. This where the real trouble begins.

A thought by itself is okay. Let's say you've lost your keys. It happens. The problem begins when you start judging the fact that you misplaced your keys. "I dislike it when I lose my keys. . . . I like it so much better when I have my keys and I can continue my busy schedule." You might go on with your thinking: "Why am I so careless? It must have been because the children were rowdy." Then you might put your thoughts into words: "Look what you made me do – I was so busy with you that I lost my keys." You might put those thoughts and emotions into physical actions by rushing around looking for the lost keys.

All this commotion stems from your reaction to a couple of misplaced keys. Let's go back to what prompted the commotion. When you had the thought, "I lost my keys," you weren't able to let go of that thought. Instead, you immediately jumped into likes and dislikes. Feeling, conflicts and frustrations are born from this dichotomy of likes and dislikes. You allowed yourself to be swept away by your judgments, your feelings, your frustrations.

But let's look at the thoughts for a moment. They arise, and by their own accord they fall away. That is, unless we cling to them. If we allow thoughts to continue their normal span, they will naturally fall away. All thoughts are subject to the universal law of impermanence, *anicca*.

For those of you who are familiar with Buddhism, you know this law of change. You accept it in many aspects of your lives. But can you apply it to the most important area of all – your mind? Can you watch thoughts and emotions as they arise in your mind? Can you allow them to naturally fade away, without clinging to them? Or do you indulge in letting the "I" grasp onto a thought, an emotion?

By their nature, thoughts are transient, unless the "I" interferes and refuses to let them go. By clinging to thoughts and emotions, the "I" prolongs the emotion-span – on and on. It is the "I" which insists on clinging to thoughts and emotions that creates non-peace.

Peace has nothing to do with the "I." It is not "my" peace. As long as you think you own peace – as long as you think, "I like my peace" – then you will not experience peace.

A friend of mine, a spiritual educator, came up with a metaphor that may help explain the process. Let's take the phrase, "I like peace." If we eliminate the "I," then we are left with "like peace." If we go further and eliminate the "like," then all that remains is peace. Peace is something that can be felt but not owned. Peace can be experienced when we eliminate our ideas of likes and dislikes about peace.

P: It sounds as though we can do something to realize this state of peace ... that we can purposely eliminate concepts of "I" and likes and dislikes.

T: No, this example is just a metaphor. Realization of peace does not come with "doing" anything with your mind, nor does it come with "not-doing." "Doing" and "not-doing" are just more concepts to cling to. Right? When you can let go of your ideas of how to obtain peace, of what to do and not do, then your mind is silent and you can experience peace. As long as your mind is rushing back and forth between likes and dislikes, then your mind is too busy to experience peace. When the mind calms and is silent, then you can realize its innate peaceful nature.

MEDITATION ON PEACE-MIND

MANY HAVE ASKED how to go about finding inner peace. Once you have recognized that

---

peace is not an induced state,
but an innate-natural state,

---

that is exactly where you begin. There is absolutely nothing to do but look within yourself and recognize peace this very moment. When you recognize peace in your mind, you have in fact already experienced peace.

If you do recognize your own peaceful moments at times, then you are already started. Never mind if this recognition is very brief. You can make this peace-moment the base from which to investigate your own mind. This can be the focal point from which to launch your investigation. And surprisingly, you will find this is also the home base to which you return.

You may find that it is not easy to come back to this peace-moment. That is not important. It is more important to decide that you want to pay attention to your own mind. We are so conditioned to looking outward that our minds have fallen into a kind of mental groove. It is difficult to rise up and leave that groove because it is easy and comfortable there. To turn outward attention inward is difficult unless one has the "will" to do it.

In your initial attempts to see peace-moments, they may be very infrequent and brief, but that is all right. It may even be that the more you try, the more difficult seeing peace or peace-moments becomes. If that is the case, just let go. Very often the awareness of peace-moments is unforeseen; it comes when you least expect it.

You may ask whether there is a specific method to "see" these peace-moments. And I would say no – not beyond the "will" to pay attention to the mind. Paying attention requires

41

no particular time or place. It goes on while you go about the daily business of living, playing, doing the one-thousand-and-one chores of what is called life. There is nothing to do beyond this. There is just something specifically you should not do and that is to let opinions, judgments and discrimination crowd your mind. The mind watching itself needs to be whole so that it can pay complete attention.

When you start discriminate, your mind becomes preoccupied with making judgments. Your mind ceases to be free. Then you cannot see or experience the peace within yourself.

In order to understand how things move in space, you must be able to see the whole panorama of space as well as the objects in it. Without space, objects cannot have motion. Objects may be affected, but the space will never be affected. The objects may disintegrate in space, but the space remains.

Your home base – the peace-nature of the mind – is just like physical space outside your body. Within you is the space of consciousness where thoughts and emotions move about. As with the outside space, it is because of this space-mind that thoughts and feelings can arise freely and also cease freely. If your mind is already crammed, there is no room for anything to arise in it.

If you can "see" this space clearly in yourself, you also see what is rising and falling more clearly. At first, you may notice only the falling – because it is more obvious. You will find yourself less involved with your own emotions and thus more at your home base. And the more you are at your home base, the more at peace you will be with yourself and with the world.

You may not have found perfect peace as yet, but at least you will find a breathing space in yourself, a respite. This is the time you learn to be friends with your own mind and your emotions. You will find that you no longer wrestle with them as before. The beautiful part is that you will find yourself loosening up inside. This loosening up may not appear important to you, but actually this first step is always the most important. When you are not in a tightly bound, self-inflicted tangle, you can look at yourself more objectively.

Never mind, if you do not see the rising. There is time for everything. Even when you "see" the falling away, you will notice a change. You will already experience peace. Keep on "experiencing" this peace as you would experience a good cup of coffee or a scoop of ice cream. After a while, you will find that you can "experience" your emotions without getting involved in them. Since you are more at home base, you will find that your feelings are in and of themselves fleeting.

For example, you may be surprised to find that feelings do not stay for a long time without your own invitation and your clinging to them. You will also see that they are part of the natural phenomena of the mind. In Buddhism, all phenomena are impermanent, are not of the self, and are themselves the basis of suffering.

Becoming aware of your feelings in this way is like discovering a new friend. When you realize that thse transient feelings have no power of their own, they cease to threaten you. This realization gives you a positive feeling, because you are no longer overwhelmed.

As you find out more about yourself in this way, you will also find that you reside more and more in your own peace home base. You will also realize this peace has always been there. It is just that you were so engrossed in trying to get rid of your frustrations that you had neither the time nor the skill to see this peace that is already there. In fact, peace-mind has been there all along for you to rediscover.

The path to inner peace is quite simple. You complicate it by thinking that the method should be difficult. You are conditioned to achieving this, accomplishing that. Your mind is in perpetual motion. Of course, you must earn a living, feed your family, make friends, take your children to school. That is the business of living. But if you perpetuate this frantic mode as the mode of your search for peace, you won't find peace.

What we are concerned with is slowing down ... so you can understand yourself, and experience what is already there. When you are already at the home base, do you need to do anything to stay there?

**You need only to wake up and realize
you have always been home.**

We must be aware that this kind of meditation is a way of investigating and understanding ourselves, of awakening to our actual state of mind, to all the mental formations that arise and fall. It is an entrance to ourselves. We will discover the bad things as well as the good, but in the end the investigation will pay off. For now we can find an opportunity to discover our own wondrous inner depths and draw upon the essence of what is the best in us.

SILENT MIND

J: I still don't understand how we can make the mind silent.

T: You must realize that you cannot make the mind silent. The more you try to silence the mind purposefully, the more you tie yourself up in knots. The more you try to quiet your mind, the more you propel it into activity. If you try to vanquish your mind, you'll find that the action of subduing is itself disquieting. You see, a mind that is already unquiet cannot deal with a nonquiet mind. This vicious cycle perpetuates a continuous state of frenzy.

M: What do you mean by silent mind? If there is no action in the mind, aren't we paralyzed? How can we function?

A silent mind is not a dead or static mind. A mind is dead or static when it is dulled with ignorance of oneself. In Buddhism, this ignorance is called *avijja*. Self-conceit, anger, greed and confusion cloud the mind. The mind may be active with greed, hatred and anger, but that mind is dead to the world and to others. Totally wrapped up in its own confusions, that mind is insensitive to the needs of others. This is a true paralysis of the mind, which renders it unable to open up to others. A truly silent mind, on the other hand, is alert and sensitive to its surroundings. This is because a silent mind is devoid of judging, clinging or rejecting. The silent mind is free from hatred, anger, jealousy, confusion and conflict.

J: It sounds so beautiful! How can we achieve this silent mind?

The mind is silent when it transcends the duality of liking and disliking. Generally we perceive the world through a conceptual framework based on a dualistic way of thinking. As soon as we perceive something, we judge it. Let's say we judge that it is good. As soon as we judge something as being good, then anything opposing it automatically becomes bad. We constantly divide our conceptual world in this polarized manner; we set up good and evil, beauty and ugliness, right and wrong, according to our own standards.

M: But we have to discriminate in order to function in everyday life. I'm not going to eat a rotten apple. It would make me sick. I have to judge this apple rotten, that one ripe and good to eat.

Of course you need to make judgments to function in this world. You need to recognize a good apple from a bad one. This is rational, not emotional, judgment. But usually we don't stop at making rational judgments. We go on to impose our emotional judgment of likes and dislikes onto our perceptions. We dislike a rotten apple, don't we? Therefore, we cling to our dislike of it.

Suppose someone offers you a rotten apple. How would you feel?

M: I would be annoyed.

Yes. And if they gave you a big beautiful apple?

M: I'd be delighted.

Do you see how your emotions are built up around your own likes and dislikes? When you find something that appeals to you – an idea, a person or a thing – then you want to cling to it, to possess that idea, person or thing. You become caught up in the duality of beauty versus ugliness, good versus evil, on and on.

Let's go back to your big, beautiful apple. Suppose someone snatches your beautiful apple away?

M: I'd be very annoyed.

There you see. Where's the problem?

M: Oh, you mean the apple is not the problem, but we are?

Exactly. Apple is just apple, good or rotten. You can take it or leave it. You can make a rational judgment about it. But our problem is that we make emotional judgments instead. This is what we need to be clear about.

When we make emotional judgments, we set up ripples in our minds. These ripples cause larger ripples and soon a storm is brewing. This storm disturbs the mind. In all this we lose touch with the silence in the mind, the peace within. It is only when we can calm these ripples that the mind can reside in its own silence, its own equanimous state. When the mind can rest in its own stillness it can see things as they are. I call this silent mind, "peace-mind."

If we don't allow the mind to be silent, we make emotional judgments and then we get into trouble. Here is where the battle starts, within ourselves and outside of ourselves.

J: Oh, I see. We cling to what we judge to be good, right or beautiful, and reject its opposite.

Yes, you've got it.

J: But how do we break out of this duality?

Remember, duality is a creation of our conceptual minds. We love to cling to what we have created. The duality we create becomes a personal possession. "I" want to hold onto "my" idea of right, "my" idea of beauty, "my" idea of good. Our minds become rigid, and we end up looking at the world through narrow blinders.

J: How can we free ourselves from this fixation?

By being mindful. When you are mindful of yourself judging in that moment, the judging will stop. Once you stop judging, "seeing things as they are" will follow naturally. Eventually, you will become more equanimous; your mind will stop and look instead of running around in circles. When the mind is busy judging, clinging and rejecting, it has no space for anything else. Only when you stop discriminating can you see things as they are, and not as you think they are or want them to be. This is the only way to transcend the duality of likes and dislikes.

Once we transcend duality, once we break through the boundaries of our own conceptual framework, then the world appears expanded. It's no longer limited by our tunnel vision. When the bondage is broken, then whatever has been dammed up within us all these years has a chance to emerge. Love – and along with it, compassion, sympathetic joy and equanimity – come forth and bring sensitivity to others.

In the past, our energy was sapped by conflict, frustration, anger, rejection, etc. This conflict was exhausting. Now free from conflict, we can redirect ourselves toward harmonious living and meaningful relationships with others. Only then does life become worth living, because now we can experience fully each moment in its freshness. We can also see our relationships with others in a totally new light. Now we can truly live in harmony.

T: The Four Noble Truths are the cornerstone of Buddhism. Understanding them helps us in daily life. The First Noble Truth is *dukkha*, or suffering. The Second Noble Truth is *samudaya*, or craving. The Third Noble Truth is *nirodha*, or cessation of suffering. The Fourth Noble Truth is *magga*, the Eightfold Noble Path, leading to cessation of suffering.

M: *When I hear the First Noble Truth, that life is suffering, I think Buddhism is a pessimistic, negative philosophy.*

Yes, some people misunderstand it that way. But this is because the teaching has not been fully understood. When *dukkha* is translated as suffering, it is understood as gross physical suffering. But in truth, *dukkha* can be experienced on many levels; the actual meaning of *dukkha* encompasses the whole range of human experience from very subtle dissatisfaction to gross misery. *Dukkha* is the inescapable fact of old age, illness and death. It is being separated from what one likes, enduring what one dislikes.

At the most profound level *dukkha* is the failure to understand the insubstantiality of all things. Everything is insubstantial; nothing is concrete, nothing is tangible. To be ignorant of or go against the natural state of impermanence is itself suffering.

Buddhism seems negative only if one looks at the First Noble Truth in isolation. But if you look at the Four Noble Truths collectively, you will find that they are positive, because the three other noble truths show the way out of suffering.

M: *But how do we incorporate the Four Noble Truths into daily life?*

T: That is not difficult. To begin with, you have to see *dukkha* in its entirety before you can see your way out of it. You don't have to be in physical or mental agony to understand *dukkha*. It is everywhere around you. Right now, how do you feel about the pounding noise next door?

[*Noisy construction work was going on at a neighbor's house.*]

M: *I feel irritated because I want to have a peaceful experience and listen to you and learn what you are talking about. In fact, I'm trying to eliminate the noise from my consciousness, but I can't.*

Because that is not the way to solve the problem.

M: *The noise annoys me and I want to stop it. I have a craving for the workers to stop.*

Well then, you have already set up a *desire* that the noise should stop. How did the desire arise? It arose from your dissatisfaction with the current situation. In other words, you desire a peaceful circumstance right now. Since you can't have it, you are annoyed. There is already aversion in your mind.

Suppose you were in the midst of doing something that was very important to you. Then this aversion might flare up into overt anger, hatred or even violence. Aversion is already a stressful state. Anger, hatred and violence bring on even greater stress and suffering, both to oneself and to others. These are the truths that we have to face in every moment of our daily lives. But we are not aware of this aversion and suffering. We blame our *dukkha* on someone or something else.

This lack of awareness is called *avijja*, or ignorance – that is, ignorance about the Four Noble Truths. This ignorance is described as an unawakened state. If you wake up to your own state of mind, right now, you will see what is happening there.

Can you look into your own mind this very moment and see what is happening there?

M: *See what?*

What happens to the annoyance.

M: *When I become aware of the annoyance, it sort of lessens.*

As soon as you become aware of the annoyance, the

aversion fades away. It resolves in the mind.

M: Yeah, a little bit.

Is it still there?

M: You mean the annoyance? It's much less. It is still there but it is much less now. [laughter] I see. So it's not a question of putting the irritation out of your mind. It is a question of accepting the fact that your mind is irritated and annoyed.

You are right. The issue is not the noise. It is *your reaction* to the noise. You have to deal with yourself first before you deal with the noise. Now, what are you going to do about it?

M: That's my next question. We have a number of choices. We can move away from the noise. We can ask the workers to stop hammering. We can continue to sit here and try to maintain our awareness of the noise in order to minimize the irritation.

You have to be clear. Is it the awareness of the noise or the awareness of your own state of mind?

M: Awareness of my own state of mind regarding it.

Right. There are many situations in life when you will not be able to eliminate external factors. We cannot eliminate or control most of the external factors in our lives, but we can do something about ourselves. You begin with yourself. Since you are born with a free will, it is absolutely up to you what you want to do with yourself.

M: Are you saying that since I cannot make the noise go away, I can just choose to accept it?

You must understand the difference between accepting things blindly and accepting them intelligently. Acceptance can be complete only when you harbor no judgments.

Now let's go back to the Four Noble Truths. Your dissatisfaction with the noisy circumstances is the First Noble Truth of Suffering – *dukkha*. Your desire or craving for peace is the Second Noble Truth – *samudaya* – which is the cause of *dukkha*. Now as soon as you look within yourself and re-solve the annoyance, you are free from the cycle of desire-aversion-desire. Aren't you ? Now look into yourself again.

M: The annoyance is already gone! It is amazing that you had to bring the noise back again into my awareness.

Let's look at what we've been going through. You have seen that it is possible to break the cycle of suffering by merely looking into your own state of mind. This in actual fact is mindfulness of the mind, which is the basis of *sati-patthana* meditation in Buddhism.

Do you see now how practicing mindfulness can lead to the end of suffering?

M: No, not yet. How does mindfulness relate to the acceptance of the noise?

The acceptance is the result of mindfulness. The act of mindfulness is a transcending act. It transcends likes and dislikes, and purifies our vision. We see things as they are. When we see or hear things as they really are, acceptance comes naturally.

M: You are aware of the noise. You get rid of the clinging to silence and you accept the noise. You accept that the noise will be part of the experience.

There is not even "you" there. There is just acceptance.

M: Aahh.

The acceptance comes from the freedom of the mind in the moment. As soon as the cycle is broken, you no longer feel annoyed. When your mind frees itself emotionally from the noise, it assumes a state of equanimity and acceptance.

M: You're not expecting it to stop and you're not expecting it to get louder.

That's right. You are free of any conceptualizing regarding the noise. You arrive at a point where you can just hear it as it is. With that hearing of the noise as it is, acceptance is already part of the situation. You can't force yourself to accept it. That's why I am very careful using these words. When you say, "I accept," that usually means . . .

M: I am in control.

Yes, that's right and that doesn't really solve the problem. The kind of acceptance we are talking about is a natural spontaneous absorbing of the environment, being one with it.

M: Oh, I see. There ceases to be a division between the noise and my experience of the noise. So there is nothing to accept or be annoyed about.

Right. Now let us go back to your experience right this minute. Are you still irritated by the noise?

M: Not anymore. I'm completely free of it. You mentioned mindfulness being the foundation of meditation. How does that work?

Yes. Mindfulness of one's own mind at any moment is part of the practice of *satipatthana*. In this particular instance, your own mindfulness of annoyance is contemplation of the First Noble Truth – *dukkha*. Your mindfulness of the desire for peace and of clinging to silence, which is the cause of *dukkha*, is contemplation of the Second Noble Truth – *samudaya*. The moment that you become free of the annoyance is *nirodha* – the Third Noble Truth. In this case, the cessation of suffering is momentary, so it can be called *tadanga nirodha*.

M: And the Fourth Noble Truth?

When you practice mindfulness you are in fact practicing *magga*, the Noble Eightfold Path. You are making the right effort, called *samma vayama*, to be mindful, called *samma sati*, of your annoyance. As a result, your mind becomes collected, which is called *samma samadhi*. When you transcend your dislike of the noise and your irritation ceases, at that moment you are able to regard the sound as it is. This is called *samma ditthi* or right view. It is *samma sankappa*, right thinking, when you are not expecting it to get louder. You are able to verbalize the situation with proper insight, called *samma vaca*. Now do you still feel like running away from the noise?

M: Not anymore. At first I did. I might have said or done something nasty if I had had the chance.

But you didn't and that is *samma kammanta*, right action.

M: You mean no action in this context is right action?

Yes. So you can see how by practicing mindfulness with equanimity in daily life, one is already applying the Four Noble Truths and integrating the Noble Eightfold Path as living meditation.

UNITY OF THE NOBLE EIGHTFOLD PATH

IN BUDDHISM, the Noble Eightfold Path is the guide to the attainment of liberation. If it is to be understood and incorporated into our daily lives, it must be viewed in terms of unity of mind, speech and action. The Path can be explored in such great detail that one could get lost in digressions. To avoid that, we take a practical, accurate and holistic view of the Path. We look at it in terms of wisdom, ethical conduct and concentration, or – in Pali – *panna, sila* and *samadhi*.

WISDOM *(PANNA)*
1. Right understanding *(samma ditthi)*
2. Right thinking *(samma sankappa)*

ETHICAL CONDUCT *(SILA)*
3. Right speech *(samma vaca)*
4. Right action *(samma kammanta)*
5. Right livelihood *(samma ajiva)*

CONCENTRATION *(SAMADHI)*
6. Right effort *(samma vayama)*
7. Right mindfulness *(samma sati)*
8. Right collectedness *(samma samadhi)*

Even these three aspects of the Path, although identified separately for clarification, are not separate. In actual practice, with proper understanding, *sila, samadhi* and *panna* are assimilated in each moment, in every thought, word or deed.

Take, for instance, *sila*, or ethical conduct. How does one refrain from wrong speech and action? First of all, what is right speech and wrong speech? Are they not relative to time, place and person? Is there such a thing as absolute right and absolute wrong? We can go on and on without coming to a definite conclusion, and by so doing we veer away from ourselves – that is, from our minds.

The purpose of *sila* is to refrain from hurting others by

way of harmful speech and action – but how much restraint
we can impose on ourselves at all times? We react to our environment in such a habitual way that we may already have
hurt others before we realize what has happened in the
mind. This is because we are conditioned to neglect our own
minds in our daily life. Our attention is almost always directed outward. This preoccupation with the outer world is
what we have to transcend.

   Although we are dealing with verbal and physical acts,
all of these originate from the mind itself. The actions of the
mind, speech and body occur in such rapid succession that
there seems to be no interval in between. As soon as a
thought has arisen, we find ourselves speaking or doing
something. We find that we cannot control speech and bod-
ily behavior fast enough to refrain from harmful speech and
action. But *sati* (mindfulness) on the mind renders it alert to
its own actions of speech and body.

   How do we redirect our attention to our own mind?
This was the Buddha's purpose in laying out the path of
mindfulness. The objective of cultivation of the mind is to
learn to break the habitual preoccupation with the external
world so that we become more aware of what is happening
in us, in our own minds, as we go on in life. As soon as
mindfulness, *samma sati*, occurs, we find that the mind acts
no more; it stops like a witness to watch the inner state.
When this watching becomes a constant habit, second nature, the cycle of reacting mindlessly to the environment is
broken. In this moment of breakthrough, "seeing" or
"awareness" occurs: crystal-clear perception of things as
they are, of people, situations and things properly in perspective, free of discriminations, likes and dislikes. From this
new insight thre follows right thinking, right speech and
right action, relative and appropriate to each specific circumstance and instance. Then the question of what is absolutely right or absolutely wrong no longer arises.

   Thus, in terms of the Noble Eightfold Path, as soon as

we pay attention to our mind, there is already *samma vayama* (effort) and *samma sati* (mindfulness). When *samma sati* is full and complete, the mind enters instantaneously into *khanika samadhi* (momentary concentration), which brings forth *pañña* (wisdom). Wisdom sees things in the right perspective, *samma ditthi*. Wisdom brings *samma sankappa* (right thought); and thereby *samma vaca* (right speech), *samma kammanta* (right action) and *samma ajiva* (right livelihood.)

Hence it is possible in every conscious moment that *sila, samadhi* and *pañña* are all three incorporated in our daily business of living – while we eat, work, play and struggle. In short, our life itself becomes the Noble Eightfold Path.

MS: You have translated samma samadhi *as "one-pointedness of mind" or "right concentration." Isn't, textually speaking,* samma samadhi *an absorption in the four* jhanas? *One-pointedness of mind can be right- or wrong-pointedness of mind and, therefore, may not fit the true understanding of* samma samadhi. *This distinction becomes important when we talk about meditation and concentration in daily life.*

T: Well, *samma samadhi* is generally translated as one-pointedness of mind or right concentration. But when it is expounded in detail it is described in two categories: *jhanic* absorption as in *samatha* meditation, and *khanika samadhi* (momentary concentration) as in *vipassana* meditation of the dry-visioned (*sukkha-vipassaka*) path of daily life.* Thus I personally think it should not be translated as absorption in the four *jhanas* only. In this I am following the commentarial rather than the canonical tradition.

You are correct, though, that one-pointedness of mind can be of the right or wrong kin, because the power of the concentrated mind is enormous and can be directed toward harmful activities if not governed by wisdom. This is exactly

---

*See Jayasuriya, W.F.: *The Psychology and Philosophy of Buddhism,* pages 162-164

why the Path sould be understood and practiced in a holistic manner. If you take meditation out of the context of the Noble Eightfold Path, without morality or the pursuit of wisdom (*pañña*), then naturally it cannot be called *samma samadhi*. In the case of meditation in daily life, what is important is the arising of wisdom (*pañña*) as a sequel of mindfulness in the moment as a preventive to harmful thoughts, words, action or livelihood.

A traditional elaboration of the Noble Eightfold Path
is given at the end of this book (see page 108).

M: *What really scares me about meditation is the idea of becoming completely without thought, completely mindless.*

T: Let me clarify your usage of "mindless" and "completely without thought." Mindless in your context would mean that the mind is totally absent, without any consciousness, a vacuum. This is not possible. Without consciousness we would be dead. "Completely without thought" means consciousness exists, but no thoughts are present. This is possible in meditation, but only under certain conditions. In some forms of sitting meditation it is possible to reach a state where the mind is absolutely quiet, one-pointed and absorbed in itself. This is called *jhanic samadhi*. In this meditative state, the person cannot function.

M: *I don't think I could be completely without thought. It sounds like I would become like a zombie.*

It is only a temporary state, which one comes out of. But we have been talking about another way of meditating, a way that sidesteps the problems of *jhanic samadhi*. If you practice mindfulness in everyday life as you have experienced just now, you do not go through absorptive states.

M: *It sounds like daily-life meditation is a more active process than I had thought. How does the mindfulness process relate to this kind of meditation?*

Let's be clear. The process is active whether one is in formal meditation or in a daily-life situation. In the sitting practice, although the body is stationary, the mind is actively watching; it is mindful of the body or the mind. Meditation is a mental discipline that ultimately leads the mind to a purified state.

M: *In daily-life meditation, is the mind actively watching itself through a state of no thought?*

Yes. When your mindfulness is at its peak, you can experience states where thoughts fall away. But the no-thought state lasts for only a split second. You experience a heightened awareness that is one-pointed as well as absolutely quiet. This momentary one-pointedness of the mind is called *khanika samadhi*. Although it is not as prolonged as the *samadhi* states in sitting meditation, *khanika samadhi* has the same intensity and quality. In *khanika samadhi*, thoughts fall away and the mind arrives at its purest state.

M: If thoughts fall away, does it mean that no "I" exists in that moment?

Yes, but only momentarily.

M: If no "I" exists in that moment, what does exist? What happens in that moment of no thought?

When split-second *samadhi* occurs, in that moment there is no thought, but only an absolutely pure and heightened consciousness. It is at that moment that *panna* or insight awareness arises. The person experiences pure vision, *ditthi visuddhi*. In Pali, *ditthi* means view and *visuddhi* means purity. So, it means pure vision.

Although this experience may be brief, it is timeless and infinite; it is a moment of transformation. It is the moment when the "I" and "mine" resolve. After that moment of no thought, pure vision is followed by thought, but the thoughts, emotions and actions are not in the old habitual routine. In the moment of an absolutely still and quiet mind, pure vision (*panna* or insight), love and compassion arise from our inner depths. Subsequent thoughts and actions are tempered with love and compassion.

You see, meditation does not make you into an inert, unthinking, unfeeling person, my dear. In fact, meditation brings out the best in you – love, warmth and sensitivity to all beings.

The practice of mindfulness, whether within the sitting

meditation or in this daily-life meditation, is an active, on-going process. In the sitting practice, although the body is stationary, the mind is actively watching and mindful of the body or the mind. Likewise, in meditation in daily life, the mind is actively watching itself regardless of posture and time. The mental discipline involved in each form is what is most crucial and ultimately leads the mind to its purified state. It is not the postures that lead to enlightenment, though postures are useful in helping the mind to quiet itself. If you understand this clearly, you can meditate anywhere and anytime.

INNER RETREAT

L: I've just finished a retreat at a meditation center and I am having some difficulty adjusting to the outside world. It was so tranquil in the center that I find it very difficult to cope with the sights and sounds and all the confusion outside. How can one cope with the transition?

T: Your experience is not unusual. Many people find themselves in the same kind of situation when they first leave a meditation center. In the retreat, conditions for peace and quiet are established, and meditation can be practiced without disturbance. While you are in the retreat, you become temporarily conditioned to these quiet circumstances. So when you come out, you find the bombardment of the sights and sounds difficult to handle.

L: How can one better cope with the transition?

Let's look at how your mind functions inside and outside the retreat. When you were in the retreat, you were practicing mindfulness intensively. Your mindfulness was in a very high gear. When you came out, you probably left the mindfulness behind, didn't you?

L: Ha! I actually did.

There you are! As soon as you left the retreat, you changed gear. You let your mindfulness go and you were back to your old unmindful state. When you are suddenly faced with the confusion in the outside world, you find it difficult to handle. The difficulty arises because you separate meditation from daily experience. Actually, the mindfulness you have learned in the retreat should equip you better to face the outside world.

L: How's that?

Well, first you must overcome the impression that mindfulness can only be practiced in the retreat and at a

particular time and place. This conditioning renders it difficult for anyone to bridge the gap between the retreat and
the outside world. In the retreat, you have learned to be
mindful sitting cross-legged with your eyes closed. Now
that you are out of the retreat you can practice the same kind
of mindfulness, but you have got to be able to do it with
your eyes open, while you deal with a myriad of problems
and bombardments.

L: Isn't that difficult?

Nothing is too difficult if you know how. Probably the
first thing you learned in the meditation retreat was how to
be in the present moment. You can also practice that outside.
You can be mindful of everything you do – cooking, wash-
ing up, bathing, driving, walking. You can be mindful of just
about anything.

Not only that, but in the retreat you invariably learn to
watch your mind like a witness, without likes and dislikes.
In daily life you can watch your mind like a witness in the
same way. You can watch your aversions to sights and
sounds as they come to you. Let them come and let them go.
Be equanimous to your feelings about the outside world,
and your equanimity will overflow to the outside world itself as well.

As you are witness to your own reactions to the outside
world, you will also become a witness to the sights and
sounds, and not be so disturbed by them. When you become
quite good at this, you will actually be living with an inner
retreat whatever your circumstances, whether quiet or not.
All the world may go round and round, but your inner
world will be still and you will find you won't need a separate time and place to meditate.

*L: What about setting up a time to practice at home in the course of
the day?*

It is fine to do that if you can be equanimous about that

set period of practice. You see, what happens with most people is that they become dependent on that meditative practice and find they cannot function the whole day properly if they do not have the chance to sit and meditate in the morning.

L: Why is that?

It is a form of conditioning like everything else. It is like being addicted to the morning cup of coffee or tea. You can become addicted to meditation also. Although this is definitely not a bad conditioning *per se*, there are many subtleties that one must be aware of in meditation. The mind is very tricky, and one must always be aware of how the mind can be trapped.

L: Then what does one do in such circumstances?

The most important thing is to develop equanimity toward your own practice. It may be the most difficult thing to do because, like everything else, one becomes attached to the meditative practices. We learn to be equanimous with other things, but forget to be so with our own practice.

L: If we can be equanimous with our practice, will it be possible to set aside a time for meditation and yet maintain an equilibrium through out the day?

That will be possible if you can be equanimous and at the same time mindful outside the practice session. Then you can be good at meditating, both in and out of the set period.

Reflections on
Meditation

Concentration and Meditation

FOR MANY PEOPLE the act of concentration is synonymous with meditation. That is probably the reason why so
many good Buddhists are more or less satisfied with the notion that when they are doing something in a concentrated
fashion – such as reading, working, playing golf – they are
already meditating. They are partly right and partly wrong.

Actually, concentration is only a part of meditation. The
essence of meditation is to reach a higher form of understanding, *pañña*, to stretch the mind beyond the boundaries
of the intellect into the realm of the intuitive, of insight-
wisdom. In most cases, meditative disciplines require col-
lecting the mind to a one-pointed state in the initial stages.
The first method used is to train the mind to concentrate on
one single object.

If one considers the pure act of concentration one uses
in one's work or hobby, one sees that the objective of such a
feat is quite different from that of meditation. In our work or
hobby we are merely concerned with accomplishing something that is outside of us generally, like job success, winning
a game of golf, completing a scientific experiment, etc. In
meditation, however, the achievement is inward, an achievement of self-understanding and spiritual insight. In the initial
stages of meditation it may be necessary to concentrate on
objects that are external to one's mind, like on the nostrils, or
on the movement of the abdomen, until the mind is collected
at one point. This type of one-pointed collectedness also occurs while we work or play, but that's where the similarity
between concentration and meditation ends.

Concentration is pure and simple collectedness of the
mind, whereas meditation is the collected mind moving further toward the development of insight-wisdom, or *vipassana*. In meditation, the awareness of the mind automatically
shifts onto the mind itself and of its own accord focuses on
its workings and processes, ultimately leading to true self-

knowledge.

Though we may come to some form of understanding while concentrating on work and play, this type of knowledge or understanding is intellect-bound, whereas meditative knowledge is intuitive and spiritual. Therefore, the two kinds of understanding are entirely different in nature and serve completely different purposes.

In pure concentration, there is always duality in the mind – "I" and "what I am doing." There is a subject, an object and the process of doing. In other words, there is the knower, the known and the knowing. Meditation also begins with these three. But eventually the mind transcends these divisions by turning inward toward itself. The ultimate enlightenment experience is the state where the differentiation of knower, the known and the knowing ceases.

To confuse concentration with meditation leads to the difficult-to-overcome states of apathy and self-satisfaction. Thus, the concept that concentration and meditation are the same is a misunderstanding that offers us no help on the path to liberation, and may even hamper aspirants in their inner progress.

MS: You said that in the concentrated activities of daily life, such as reading or working, there is always a duality in the mind – that is, there is the knower, the knowing and the known. It seems to me that there is a distinction between concentration in an ordinary activity and absorption in an actifity like painting or making music or some other artistic endeavor where the knower, the knowing and the known seem to disappear. This grey area comes up again and again in Dhamma talks and questions. Would you elaborate on this?

T: Actually, during absorption in artistic activities like painting or making music, etc., the knower, the knowing and the known do not completely disappear. What happens is that, in these moments of heightened artistic activity, the person experiences a kind of rapture where the sense of

"I-ness" fades away to a great extent but not completely. Also, the person is still conscious of the object, be it painting or making music or whatever. Therefore, the known also does not completely disappear. I call these kinds of experiences "pseudo-spiritual incidences," because they come close to *jhanic* absorptions, but are not quite so. On the other hand, these raptures in artistic endeavors allow the artist to become more pliable and spiritual than most people.

MINDFULNESS AND AWARENESS

E: How we can practice mindfulness in daily life?

T: Generally, our awareness is very much preoccupied with the external situation, with whatever we contact through our six senses. Invariably, we react to these sensations in a habitual way. We repeat our behavior again and again, without awareness of what is happening in our minds. In Buddhism this is known as *avijja*, or ignorance. This does not mean intellectual ignorance, but specifically lack of insight into oneself.

E: But we do seem to know our own minds, don't we?

In one sense we do, but only in a sluggish manner. For example, when we go through an emotional upheaval, we are aware of it only after the incident is over. At the time of the turmoil we are lost in our confusion.

We generally focus on the external factors we think are affecting us. Take, for example, the case of eating. Our attention is focused on the food: its taste, its smell and appearance. If the food is not up to our expectations, we immediately react to it with annoyance – or even anger, if we are already in a bad mood. Then we are apt to vent our anger on anyone or anything we come into contact with.

But if we look at the situation analytically, we will see that the problem does not begin outside of us. Another person who is not concerned with that food, or who even likes it, will enjoy it without making a fuss. So the root of the problem is not in the food but in our judgmental and discriminating mind. The moment we start thinking, "I don't like it," we reject the existing situation as being unacceptable. This rejection always ends up in anger or tension in one form or another.

E: Then how do we practice awareness?

Awareness cannot be practiced.

69

E: Oh? But we hear and read so much about practicing awareness in Buddhism, don't we?

There has been some confusion between awareness and mindfulness.

E: But I always thought they were the same.

They are related, but distinct. *Sati*, or mindfulness, implies there is action of the mind. We purposely set ourselves to pay attention to our minds. We exert effort. Awareness is different.

Awareness is devoid of any action.

The mind simply "awares." There is no action here, only a collected and spontaneous awareness that just "sees." Here, mindfulness is the cause, and awareness is the effect. You cannot practice or train the effect. You can only practice something that will cause it. We have to start with mindfulness so that awareness may arise in us.

E: How do we practice mindfulness?

Normally, our minds are in constant motion, thinking, feeling, endlessly flitting from one thing to another. Because of this perpetual motion, there is little room for awareness to arise. Awareness may peek through at times, but it is too timid. It is sluggish and dull. Most often our noisy thoughts and emotions dominate the scene. The mind must get out of this perpetual cycle for awareness to arise fully.

E: How does this happen?

The mind must readjust itself, redirecting its usually externally oriented attention onto mindfulness of itself. When we redirect ourselves in this way, we replace all other mental activities with mindfulness. Rather than getting caught in all the mental activities, we are left only with "paying attention." At each single moment the mind can accommodate only one mind state. For example, we cannot be angry and be happy at the same time, can we?

E: Goodness, no.

When there is anger in our minds, there is no room for happiness. When mindfulness occupies the whole of our minds, there is no room for any thought or emotion to arise at that specific mind-moment. There is pure attentiveness. When this attentiveness is total, the perpetual roller-coaster state of the mind is broken: the mind finds a balanced footing in itself. Then awareness can arise on its own accord.

**When there is complete balance,
there is awareness.**

E: Can you relate this to the incident of eating?

Well, suppose you are used to paying attention to your mind. As soon as you see the food, and thoughts of dislike enter your mind, you will be aware of what is happening in you. When you watch your feelings of like and dislike without judgment, you will be left only with the watching. There is no chance for subsequent thoughts to arise. In short, your emotions will be stopped in their tracks instead of building up. Maybe you cannot stop your dislike of the food, but that is not important. The crucial thing is that when you are stopped in your tracks, you begin to see the situation "as it is" and not "as I want it." This "seeing" is the awareness we are talking about. Instead of reacting with anger, you can now relate to the situation in a relatively calm way and deal with it rationally, with harmony. The situation leads constructively to your own and others' satisfaction.

E: You mean awareness dispels all the confusion in you?

Yes, it does.

E: But how?

You see, in awareness the mind becomes an "all-seeing" state – which in Buddhism is called *pañña* (insight wisdom). Although we say awareness, this awareness is not just "being" aware. It is not a passive state. It brings with it a dynamic perception which cuts through all confusions in the mind.

The total external situation is revealed in its entirety with transparent clarity. When we see the world through our own confusion, the scene is very much distorted. The more confused we are, the more distorted our view of the world is. Therefore, our reactions are also distorted, and we create confusion around us. It is only when confusion is transcended by *pañña* that we have clarity in ourselves. With this clarity we can deal with the external situation in a wholesome and creative way.

In the Moment

P: Why is it that we find it so refreshing to go to a place which is totally different from what we are used to? I always find it necessary to get away from my normal life and take a break, to find a change of scene and environment. Is that quite normal?

T: I don't know whether you would call it normal or abnormal, but one can say that it is quite usual. It is quite usual for us to feel suffocated and hemmed in by our lives. One feels the need to get away from it all, to take a break, and to find new experiences to sustain oneself.

But you must also understand that it is not mainly the suffocating life situation that is driving us to seek relief temporarily, though that does help to some extent. The main reason is that one is not free in the present moment. When one is not free, one cannot experience this very moment fully and completely.

P: So one is actually seeking a diversion when one does not find satisfaction in the present. But even when one gets to a new place and finds the new experience to be exciting, the satisfaction does not last for long, because it only satisfies the senses and not the spirit.

Yes, this is true. When you get back to your original situation, you find that you are on the old treadmill again. But, come to think of it, what is it that makes you feel contented and satisfied? You can be contented and satisfied only when the mind is free from desires and clinging, for only the free mind can experience each moment fully and completely.

To a mind free from desires, free from conflicts and frustrations, each moment is fresh and new. If your mind is always burdened with conflicts and frustrations, you cannot experience the moment fully. There is no clarity or room for experience. In this sort of situation you are either living in the past or in the future; the experience of the present is only partial. You are only partly aware of the present, so to say.

You do not experience the freshness of the moment, the joy of everything you come into contact with. So you go out to seek freshness in other places, from other people, in new relationships and so on. However, the cycle continues, because the root of the problem is not in the environment but within yourself. Until that truth is properly understood and dealt with, you continue the search for satisfaction everywhere, and yet find it nowhere.

Meditation without Meditation

R: *What is sitting meditation?*

T: You purposefully quiet your mind so that you can go deeper and deeper within yourself.

R: *Then why don't you teach us sitting meditation?*

Buddhist *vipassana* meditation (insight meditation) involves four methods. First, *kaya-nupassana*, meditation on the body. For example, the in-breath and out-breath, walking, sitting and standing. Second, *vedana-nupassana*, contemplation on sensations and feelings. Third, *citta-nupassana*, contemplation on the mind. And fourth, *dhamma-nupassana*, contemplation on mental and intellectual objects.

R: *You mean all this time I have been meditating on the last three?*

What else? Yes, you have been meditating on the last three.

R: *You mean in all the struggling I have done watching my feelings and confusions, struggling with the discussions in the group and with my readings, I have been meditating all the time and never even knew I was meditating?*

This is a good way of putting it. Yes, you have been meditating without knowing that you were meditating. This is called "meditation without meditation."

R: *But why are we so stuck with the idea that to meditate we must sit in a certain way at a certain time?*

You see, institutional forms of *vipassana* meditation have become extremely popular in Asian Buddhist countries and in the West. Whatever methods the teachers and founders of these institutions may use, there is one feature common to all of them: a structured system or form within which the student of meditation learns to meditate. So meditation has become synonymous with sitting meditation.

R: But how does meditation without meditation work? I mean, how does it achieve results without our having to go through rigorous discipline?

I think you mean the rigor of the sitting meditation as a discipline. You see, the sitting is only an aid to the more important discipline of the mind. The sitting is not to train the body *per se*, but to train the mind in the art of mindfulness and in going beyond. In formal meditation you concentrate on the body at one point – either on the breath or on sensations – in order to relinquish any thoughts, feelings or intellectual activities of the mind, to help it become collected at one point. In the process you learn to watch the mind without judgment and discrimination and also learn to let go.

R: But you have been telling us the same thing: to watch the mind, to let go, etc.

Exactly. You can watch your mind while you quietly sit in the meditative posture, or you can do so while you function in your daily life. Either way is feasible, depending on your own disposition.

In the unstructured approach, you have to face yourself very often. In trying to let go, you must first of all face your own ego and pride. Nobody wants to face his or her own ego. It is too painful. It takes great mental effort to do so. In this unstructured approach, facing your own ego is itself a meditative act of the mind. It requires *sati* (mindfulness), effort, *samadhi* (collectedness of mind) and equanimity. It may not require the rigorous disciplining of the body, but it definitely requires perseverance and rigorous disciplining of the mind.

R: But what about our discussions and readings? How do they help develop insight?

In sitting meditation, you purposefully waive intellectualization by concentrating on one single point – let us say, on the breathing. However, in this less formal approach I am teaching, you use the intellect as a tool to develop insight. Reading, discussing and contemplating the Dhamma sharpen your intellect and insight. But there is a very important point here. If your efforts are only at the intellectual level, then you will only collect intellectual knowledge. This is quite different from actual experiential insight. In our discussions we have always gone beyond intellectualization of the Dhamma. We have gone into personal experience, into the nitty-gritty of life as we live and struggle through. Do you remember many times you've said: "It's impossible; I can't understand it. I can't let go of my opinions and clinging"?

R: Yes, that's right.

And many times you've said, "if I understand, I'll let go." But you found that:

**you can understand only when
you let go of intellectualization.**

R: That is correct.

You make use of your intellect only where it works. The intellect has a limit; it can only go so far. When it is exhausted, it just lets go. That is when you experience the "seeing." Then the "understanding" just hits you.

R: But there is a price for this. My goodness, I had to pay so much – all my pride, my likes and dislikes, my clinging. How I loved my clinging! I had to learn to let go of all that. It was not an easy thing. In fact, it was an enormous struggle, mind you, and sometimes agonizing.

Yes, one does not get something for nothing. But it depends on how we persevere, how willing we are to look within ourselves. We have to be brave enough to face ourselves. That is a great struggle and it takes great effort and courage to do so. But it is, in fact, an effortless effort.

R: Oh?

Yes, you are making an effort without really consciously "trying" to make an effort. In Buddhism that is called *viriya*. It can happen in daily life or in sitting meditation.

R: *You mean we are transcending ourselves during all this struggling?*

Exactly. You've been doing that without knowing you were transcending yourself. In sitting meditation, you are taught the "how-to" of letting go at each and every step of the way. The difference here is that you let go without knowing it. Your intellect just simply cannot go any further; it just lets itself go.

R: *Oh, that's why, when I try to think about the Dhamma and our discussions, I don't really understand. But later on when I stop thinking about them, the "understanding" just strikes me. It isn't my doing. It just comes like lightning out of the blue. At one point I thought your discussions were too intellectual, especially the* Abhidhamma *teachings.*

Yes, you can even make use of the dullest intellectual treatise in the Pali Canon to transcend yourself!

R: *Well, that's something new.*

Even that is not! Nothing is ever wasted, if you know how to make use of it. All of our sessions, even the *Abhidhamma* teachings, helped you stretch your mind. You were making your mind more and more elastic without knowing it. You went further than you had ever gone before. Your mind had to stretch beyond its previous rigid orbit. The more difficult the discussions, the more your mind was exercised. You may not have understood anything during those sessions, but they helped you acquire the plasticity of mind that is so essential to going beyond the mundane.

R: Yes, many times I felt lost and confused.

That was because your intellect was at work. But when the intellect reaches its limit, it just drops away. Many of you have been asking me: what is the method? What do we have to do to achieve understanding? You are so conditioned to systems and methods and to structured learning that you can't see that there is an approach without any form or structure. What have we been doing in all our sessions? All the struggling you had to do within yourselves is the means to self-understanding. Whether you call it method or non-method is irrelevant.

R: I see now. We were left very much on our own to sort things out by ourselves. No methods and no gurus.

Yes, that is the way it is. When you have a guru, you cling to your guru. When you are working with a method, you cling to your method. You become dependent on them. Then you lose the impetus to investigate freely and learn for yourself. Our approach has no strict form or structure in the practice, but all the qualities of the *bojjhanga* – the seven factors of enlightenment – are already integrated in the process we have been in.

R: What are the seven factors of enlightenment?

They are mindfulness, investigation, energy, joy, tranquillity, concentration and equanimity. You have been practicing mindfulness with perseverance within the context of daily life, which in fact has been slowly building up concentration or *samadhi*. Not only that – the act of mindfulness in daily life is also an investigative process into the nature of your own mind with equanimity.

The investigation is also taking place while you are reading, studying or discussing with the group. Remember that our discussions were not just theoretical. They dealt with how to incorporate the teachings into our lives and to see through our problems of living by using the Dhamma. We have also seen how we need the right amount of effort and energy to observe our mind, to study and investigate it. And we have found that the pursuit itself, though difficult, brings peace and joy. In this manner, our way of life itself then becomes the Path to Enlightenment. This is the practice of *dhamma-nupassana.*

Creative Living

CREATIVE LIVING

H: I have the impression that Buddhism is very individualistic in its teachings.

T: It would seem so, but we are not isolated beings. We live in society. Therefore, what affects an individual invariably affects all those around him or her. Buddhism focuses a great deal on each individual's enlightenment. Although it does not neglect the community, it has to start with the individual. When each individual is well centered and in perfect equilibrium within him or herself, he or she naturally draws others' centers into balance, and hence the community as well. In other words, a spontaneous equilibrium is created within any given situation.

H: How does this come about?

There is no magic formula for it, but two basic ingredients, patience and *pañña* (wisdom), bring forth the harmony.

H: Isn't patience also a form of passivity?

If one is patient and tolerant but does not have *pañña*, that patience and tolerance can take the form of passivity. In such a case, one can even allow oneself to be abused in many ways. This is not intelligent living. Intelligent living avoids both extremes – passivity and impulsiveness.

These days people are always in a hurry and tend to be afflicted with the disease of impatience. We are plagued with the urge to "act" instantly, to get "going," to "move," and to "do" something in haste. We leave no time to reflect, to stop, to absorb, and to let things evolve or emerge by themselves. One tends to react through one's conditioned chaotic mind – rather than acting in a cool and collected way – thus creating more chaos.

Any action without intelligence is destructive. Intelligent living means "watching" and "seeing" the right moment, the right opportunity, the appropriate situation, in which to act. In Buddhism this is known as *samma kammanta* (complete and skillful action). In short, intelligent living means skillful and creative living.

H: Then, if intelligence and patience are both relevant to skillful living, how are they related? How do they come together?

Pañña (wisdom) and patience are like two sides of a coin. If there is intelligence, then patience arises by itself. Patience without intelligence is just contrived benevolence; it doesn't last long. Sooner or later one runs out of patience. True tolerance arises only through *pañña*. You see, *pañña* brings with it the four *brahma viharas* or sublime states, namely, *metta* (unconditional love), *karuna* (compassion), *mudita* (sympathetic joy) and *upekkha* (equanimity). Only love, compassion and equanimity provide a person with true benevolence. Equanimity leaves the person concerned detached from clinging; love and compassion help the person to identify with others; and *pañña* leads the person to take the right action. All these together lead to true benevolence.

H: Well then, how does one live in harmony with others?

This is an extremely important question. It is a matter of focusing on your own equilibrium. This is the most fundamental issue. Whatever situation you are facing – whether it is personal, social, one's career, family, friends, etc. – equilibrium must start right there ... with you. If you are shaky, how can you bring others into balance? The equilibrium must start right here, within yourself. Otherwise, you will only sink the ship with your shakiness.

Only when you are completely stable and well-centered can you reach out to others' inner states. You cannot change others by purposeful and forceful means. The change, first of all, must come from within yourself. The equilibrium must start right there within you. When you have struck the right balance within yourself, this balance will pervade the whole situation and will, by itself, affect others' equilibrium. It is a spontaneous occurrence. Your own tranquillity will allow other people and situations to respond to you very naturally. We need to retain an open heart, so that whenever we do anything, our action will be out of love and compassion and nothing less. This kind of living and loving generates tremendous energy for harmonious, creative and joyful life.

LOVE AND HATE

SHE WAS JUST OUT OF COLLEGE; to know her was like a breath of fresh air. She was full of life, intelligent and pleasant, with a youthful inquiring mind. She was becoming a spiritual friend.

She told me about a person she had hated since college days. This troubled her so much that even in her dreams he was bothering her. That was why she wanted to know about love and hate.

S: *Can you explain to me about love and hate?*

T: Well, you see, love and hate are not so different. They are two aspects of our discriminating mind, like two sides of the same coin.

S: *But they feel so different.*

Yes, initially they are different, but they both arise out of our habit of discrimination, and they both lead to suffering. Whether we love or hate someone is based on our own likes and dislikes. We automatically categorize people according to our own preconceptions. When they meet our ideals and appear to be to our liking, immediately our mind starts to cling to them; and if they should fall into the category of dislike, our minds start to reject them. In this way we end up loving or hating.

S: *But how can we stop loving and hating? I find both situations equally frustrating.*

Let's think about a situation where you love a person at one time and come to hate him at another. He is the same person, so why do your feelings about him change?

S: *Probably because that person and I have changed.*

True. That means our love changes with each changing situation, and that means our feelings are not permanent, but relative to time and place.

S: Our feelings are not permanent?

Exactly. This is what the Buddha called *maya*, the illusion of the mind. Our feelings are an illusion born of our conceptual mind; they arise from the ego-self. According to Buddhism, since ego is an illusion, anything that is born of the conceptual mind is also an illusion. It has no substance, permanence or peace. That is why mundane love is fickle. That is why it can change to hate.

About a week later she came to see me again, and this time, in great excitement, she said to me:

S: I fully understand now what you said about love and hate! I met that person the other day and, to my great surprise, I found myself going up to him and even greeting him without hesitation. I don't know why, but I don't feel any animosity toward him anymore. Before, I used to hate even the sight of him. It is really such a great relief to me. I feel free now!

Let me ask you one thing: before you met this person did you have this feeling of hate in you?

S: Why, come to think of it, I didn't.

And what about now; do you still have it?

S: No.

Then, what is the difference, before and after?

Then she burst into laughter, saying:

S: Very true!

Well, you were free of this hate or love before you met him, weren't you?

S: Yes, that's right.

What did you have to do to be free like that?

S: Well, I didn't have to do anything. I was free by myself.

That's right. By ourselves we are free of either loving or hating. Only when we start to like or dislike do we become entangled in our own emotions. As soon as we come to realize that they are illusions of our own making, we become free. We are brought back to our original situation where there is neither love nor hate. Only when the mind starts to work on liking and disliking is the burden of love and hate built up and we lose that freedom temporarily.

This is a real-life example of how the cloud of *moha* (delusion), once lifted, leads to freedom and self-realization in the moment.

HAPPINESS

ONE DAY a friend found me reading Buddhism and asked,
"Are you trying to find happiness?"

T: Yes.

R: *Have you found it?*

Yes, I have.

R: *How?*

By realizing that I cannot find it.

R: *But how can that be?*

There is no such thing as a feeling of happiness that is permanent and everlasting. Those feelings of elation and pleasure that arise whenever we come across things, people or events that satisfy and please us are but momentary.

We hanker after pleasurable feelings, thinking that if we get everything we want we will be happy. When we try to find satisfaction outside of ourselves, we end up running in circles. We can never get total satisfaction from others, just as we can never provide them with it. We simply forget that others are in the same position as we are! They expect the same kind of satisfaction from you and me.

As soon as we try to find happiness, we are already on the road to unhappiness.

R: *Is there no way out?*

Yes, there is a way out. We will find happiness only when we stop looking for it.

R: *But that's difficult.*

That is the paradox. The moment we want happiness, we start to cling to it in our mind. First, we cling to our own idea of happiness. We relate to the outside world as a source of satisfaction and look outward for the things we normally associate with happiness – accumulating wealth, success, fame or power. As soon as we become attached to any idea – happiness, success or whatever – there is already some stress. Clinging is itself a stressful state, and everything that derives from it is also stressful. For example, try to clench your hand to make a fist. As soon as you start to clench your hand, you have to use energy to keep your fingers clenched tightly. When you let go of the clenching, your hand is free again.

So it is with the mind. When it is in such a state of clenching, it can never be free. It can never experience peace or happiness, even if one has all the wealth, fame and power in the world.

R: *So how do we get out of this?*

The only way is to let go.

R: Let go of what?

Your desire for happiness.

LOVE AND COMPASSION

A: What is true compassion?

T: Compassion (*karuna* in Pali), as taught in Buddhism, is one of four sublime states (*brahma vihara*) that are inherent qualities of wisdom (*pañña*). The other three are unconditional love (*metta*), sympathetic joy (*mudita*) and equanimity (*upekkha*). An act of compassion is not isolated, but is also an expression of these other qualities of wisdom.

A: Suppose you have a friend who is an alcoholic, and you want to help her. What would be the right thing to do if she refuses to take your advice?

B: Even if my own son happened to be a victim, I would suggest that he go to the hospital. I would help him all I could if he wanted to go. If not, that's it, and I would not feel angry or say anything.

Yes, if what you are saying is that we can't help someone who is not ready to be helped, that is very true. But we have to be very careful here. We have to examine our own minds very carefully. There is a fine line between equanimity and indifference. If we try to perform an act of compassion in a detached way, with no wisdom governing the act, there is danger.

B: Why is that so?

Because, first of all, only wisdom can differentiate between equanimity and indifference. A person can be very proficient in dissociating herself or himself emotionally from any situation or from people. But that kind of detachment is not true equanimity; it is only a delusion, and the delusion itself can lead to indifference and negligence. You can be led to think that so long as your duty is done, that's it; the rest has nothing to do with you. You must also differentiate between fulfilling duty with indifference and acting with love and compassion. There is a very fine line between them.

B: Then what is upekkha *or equanimity if it isn't detachment?*

Detachment is the opposite of attachment. It means disengaging or dissociating from somebody or something.

**Equanimity is that which transcends
both attachment and detachment.**

It means seeing things as they are, without clinging or rejecting. It goes beyond attachment and detachment.

B: What is the difference between equanimity and indifference?

Indifference is the result of a lack of concern, a lack of love. But

---

**equanimity is born from wisdom and love.
It is not an isolated quality in itself.**

It is part and parcel of wisdom, love, compassion and joy. Likewise, compassion is not an isolated feeling. If it were isolated, then it could probably be induced by a conditioned behavior based on the idea of compassion.

A: Then what is true compassion?

True compassion and love are spontaneous manifestations of *pañña* (wisdom). If there is *pañña*, there is already love, compassion, joy and equanimity. They are all present in a single act of compassion. That act encompasses all these qualities.

For example, in the case of the alcoholic son, wisdom would give you the insight to look at the total situation – what alcoholism is doing to your son and whether it is affecting others; what it is doing to the whole family; and the mental, social and economic misery and suffering resulting from alcoholism. You may be detached and not be affected by his refusal to take up your suggestion, but your equanimity should not turn into indifference.

There is a vast and very crucial difference between detaching yourself from your emotions and detaching yourself from the situation.

You can still be genuinely concerned and actively involved in any situation without expending your emotional resources. Your own insight into the total situation and your love for the whole family leads you to the right action in that particular situation.

B: So we could say that wisdom and love serve as checks and balances to equanimity.

Yes, that's right. Love keeps you involved in the situation; compassion leads you to identify yourself with others; equanimity helps you to transcend emotional involvement and see things objectively; and wisdom helps you identify the right solution to the problem or situation for the benefit of yourself as well as of others.

A: What about sympathetic joy? How would joy come into this integrated action?

An act is joyless if it is done on the basis of pure duty. Joy is also lacking if you help someone out of pity. Duty and pity fall short of true compassion. Joy is present only when an act is born of wisdom, love, compassion and equanimity. Such action is joyful because it is not restrained by attachment nor burdened with worries and anxieties.

Love and joy bring perseverance to compassion. One does not give up easily until some good comes out of an adverse situation. An act of joy with no emotional attachment makes the involvement itself fulfilling. This is an act born of a free mind.

B: What do you mean by a free mind?

A free mind is a mind free from fixation on anything, free even from a concept of compassion.

B: What do you mean by that?

A free mind is a mind that is purely in the present moment. Because it lacks any fixations, it can view the total situation and adapt to prevailing circumstances – then you can act accordingly.

Suppose the alcoholic is your friend. How you would act would be slightly different from your actions toward a son. For the latter, you have a far greater moral responsibility than for a friend. Furthermore, your behavior would change according to your standing and relationship with that friend, his attitude, receptivity, etc. Many factors would determine how much you could be involved. On the other hand, if you have a sick child, you would not hesitate to put the child in the hospital, whether the child appreciates your decision or not. Every situation is unique and no fixed rule can be applied to all situations. The only criterion that the Buddha set was that one should act on what would benefit oneself and the other person.

B: So, there are no hard and fast rules for compassion?

The real reason we are having this discussion is that I am very concerned that any generalization I make might be taken as a guideline for action, even in the name of compassion. A fixed idea or guideline for action may not work for every situation.

Fixation leads to conditioning; every time you meet with a similar situation, you react in the same conditioned way, even though there may be differences in the situation. The mind must be free from any fixation; only then can true compassion arise. Every situation we face is unique and different from any other. Each situation has to be dealt with differently according to the needs and benefits of that particular situation. Without clear insight, if your action proves disastrous, you and others may suffer needlessly.

Equanimity and Indifference

One friend always drops in to visit me for a Dhamma discussion when he's in town. He is a devout Buddhist who has been studying and practicing the Dhamma in Sri Lanka with his Abbot teacher for many years. My friend had written me that he wanted to discuss my article on Love and Compassion. He launched into the subject as soon as he arrived.

G: I was quite struck by the piece "Love and Compassion" and I am very glad you wrote about it, because it is one of the problems I am actually facing right now with my teenage son. It is very true that when you have studied the Dhamma, you learn to detach yourself from others, but it is, as you said, very difficult to differentiate between equanimity and indifference. And very often we confuse the two. I find that when I detach myself, I also withdraw from people.

T: Yes, when we first study the Dhamma and learn to apply it to our own lives, we start by learning to detach ourselves, to let go. This is because we are so conditioned, mentally and emotionally, to cling to everything that relates to us. We learn to distance ourselves from the situation so that, instead of being absolutely immersed and caught up in it, we can look at it more objectively.

G: Like becoming a witness?

Yes, initially we must learn to be a witness and not be emotionally involved. We need to be objective, to see the situation as it is, without bias.

But in so doing – unless we have very astute guidance – we may end up detaching ourselves all too thoroughly. The detachment may overtake other feelings, like concern for and interest in the welfare and benefits of others. This may lead to psychological dissociation from the person because we can falsify our satisfaction and assume that we have done our duty and that there is nothing further to be done.

94

G: *That is so true. I find it very difficult to impress on my son what I think is in his best interest. I have become somewhat detached now, since he does not really respond. I thought I had done my duty and it was up to him to take it from there. If he didn't, then what could I do? I used to think that way. Now, I see that this is not desirable.*

Yes, when we withdraw in one way we also tend to withdraw in other ways.

G: *Why does it happen like that?*

This also is a kind of conditioning. Previously, we were conditioned to cling to everything. When we study the Dhamma, we are taught to "uncling" or let go; however, instead of clinging to all sorts of things, we now cling to the idea itself of letting go. So we become conditioned to the opposite extreme. We let go of virtually everything. Thus, when we are faced with a situation we tend to react by letting go of both the situation and the people. Even letting go can become a habit.

G: *A habit?*

You see, the mind is a peculiar thing. It is used to being fixed on something – past experiences and memories, past learning, ideas, etc. Because of this, we cannot experience each moment without attachment to anything. We even cling to the best of Dhamma ideas.

The idea of letting go is also a concept. This concept is useful when we begin to study the Dhamma, or when we practice meditation. But eventually we become so proficient at detachment that we don't realize we are clinging to yet another concept. From the concept of self we switch to the concept of non-self, the idea that "it has nothing to do with me." This leads to disinterest and lack of concern for others.

As a result, you may unconsciously close your mind as well as your heart even to those closest to you. This creates a barrier between you and those in your life.

G: Is this what you mean by indifference?

Yes, it is. From detachment, we unwittingly move on to indifference. Mind you, this is not purposeful indifference; there is no intention behind it. It's simple conditioning. So long as the mind responds to people and situations in any conditioned way, love and compassion have no space to evolve.

G: How does love evolve then?

Love evolves only in a mind that is totally free, free from fixation on any idea – even the idea of letting go. We have to learn to free ourselves from the idea of letting go.

G: But how do we free ourselves from this concept?

By mindfulness of the moment. Let me stress this. As soon as you realize that you are clinging to the idea of letting go, you will drop the letting go. In that moment of "dropping" you are free.

There is a Zen parable about a student holding a pot in each hand. When the Master saw him, he shouted, "Drop it!", and the student dropped one pot. Again the Master commanded, "Drop it!", and the student dropped the other pot. Again the Master shouted, "Drop it!", and the student became enlightened. Everything dropped from his mind. He became absolutely free. At that moment of absolute freedom the pupil experienced Truth.

When we realize that we are conditioned to letting go, we spontaneously transcend the conditioning. We stop clinging to the idea of letting go of our concern for and interest in others.

Only in moments of complete freedom from either attachment or detachment can *upekkha* (equanimity) transcend both states of mind.

Only then can insight arise spontaneously as to what is

the best approach to the situation. If the situation needs our concern, we give it; if it needs our interest, we give it; if our action or intervention is necessary, we do not hesitate. We let go and pick up at the same time.

G: Could you explain a little more?

It is important to let go of clinging to your fixed ideas – to self, or to the desire to change others, for example. But at the same time, you need to pick up the threads of life. In short, make your actions into pure acts – straight from the heart.

For example, in the case of a child who has not come of age, indifference on the part of parents is very undesirable – even dangerous. Children do not have sufficient knowledge and maturity to decide many things on their own. They require our continued concern and interest. So long as our acts do not arise out of egoism, and we have enough insight into the needs of our children, we can reach out to them. But if the idea of "letting go" creates a barrier within ourselves, we will be paralyzed. We have, first of all, to deal with our own inner problems, our desire to control. Then we can deal effectively with those outside.

G: But what about being a witness? If you are a mere witness you will not be concerned or involved.

That is true. Initially you need to learn to be a witness – to detach yourself emotionally from situations. But being a witness is only a phase in learning to be objective. When we have learned to be objective, we have to step back into the drama of life again.

G: But won't we be caught up again in the same old cycle of affairs?

Yes, that is a danger. If you have not gained any insight by your withdrawal, you may return to the same vicious cycle. But if you have really understood how to "let go and pick up at the same time," you won't get tangled up again.

You see, when you step back into the drama, you step back differently. Now, you act with clear understanding rather than fear or ignorance. Previously, you looked at the situation through your ego – you saw everything through filters. It was impossible to see the entire situation when you wanted to control the situation. Before, it was more important to justify your ego-hood. Now, after stepping back and removing the filters, you can see clearly the whole panorama of what is happening around you.

The more freedom you have in the moment, the more clarity you have about the situation. This clarity brings with it a sensitivity and compassion for others which keeps you involved, even if they don't respond immediately. You can persevere in your search for a way to benefit others, because you are not emotionally burdened. The act of involvement itself becomes joyful because it is a free act, an act of pure love and spontaneity. You are part of the whole; you are no longer isolated from others. You are connected to them without losing yourself in their problems. You stand free, yet you are not apart. That is true equanimity.

SENSE PLEASURES

SDD: I have just read something by a well known Buddhist teacher on sense pleasures and how they are the scourge of human beings. The teacher talks about how clinging to sense pleasures creates problems in society.

T: It is true that there is excessive indulgence in sense pleasures. No doubt, modern civilization has become too preoccupied with them and allowed itself to be enslaved by them. Let us look objectively at the root cause of the problem. Otherwise, we fall into the trap of rejecting the sense world and escaping from it, and in the end this is the same as being enslaved by the senses. It is possible to be bound up in rejecting the sense world.

SDD: How is that?

If you think preoccupation with the sense world is the root cause of the human problem, you may feel a sense of guilt where sensual enjoyment is concerned. You may even be afraid to experience sensual pleasures. This can lead to escapism and phobias if you are not careful.

SDD: Then what is the solution to this?

Craving after sense pleasures is primarily due to insecurity and not recognizing craving in ourselves. We don't know what we are lacking, so we look outside ourselves. We try to fill our emotional vacuum with all kinds of diversions. And, of course, with the rampant commercialism, the handiest thing is to indulge in all kinds of new experiences that cater to the senses. But invariably we find that there is no end to indulgence and pleasure-seeking. There is no lasting and absolute satisfaction from these sense pleasures because we are not free in the moment.

SDD: Why is that so?

The mind, in its state of insecurity, needs to cling to

something – material possessions, sense pleasures, distractions, wealth, fame, success or just about anything on earth – in order to fill the emotional vacuum. Actually, all these give us is a false sense of security or temporary satisfaction.

SDD: How does one deal with insecurity?

There is only one way to deal with insecurity.

SDD: What is that?

It is to arrive at the understanding that security cannot be found anywhere or in anything.

SDD: Oh? Why is that?

It is the search for security itself that makes the mind insecure; the mind is so bound up with the search that it is not free to experience what can be found in the present moment. We tend to project ourselves into the future, so we cannot live fully in the present; we experience the present only partially. Thus we do not experience the freshness of each moment. But if each moment is experienced fully with every encounter, the beauty and the joy that day-to-day surroundings bring become so obvious that there is no need to look for satisfaction elsewhere.

SDD: But how does one learn to live in the present moment?

It all goes back to being mindful in the moment.

SDD: Mindful of what? Is it on the body or on what you are doing?

Mindfulness on the body does help you to exist in the present moment, but the most crucial thing is to realize your own freedom in the moment. If you start to want this and want that, thinking about the past or thinking about how you are going to enjoy the future, you are not free. Your present moment is preoccupied with the wanting and as a result your natural freedom in the moment is lost.

SDD: You mean, we are naturally free but make ourselves "un-free?"

Yes, it is as though you were being tied by with an invisible rope, by no one but yourself.

SDD: What you mean is, when you realize that there is no such thing as a rope tying you, you are already free!

That's exactly it. You are back to your natural freedom in the moment, and you can experience relationships afresh, in ordinary living. Even very mundane things become so fulfilling that there is no need to search for freedom elsewhere or to be dependent on new experiences and sense pleasures. You see, this natural freedom in us is the only permanent thing, because it is the innate essence of our being; it is life's natural gift. Everything outside of ourselves is contrived and unsatisfactory.

So, to be free of sense pleasure is neither to cling to nor run away from it, but to learn to be free in yourself. From this premise of freedom in yourself, the sense world will neither threaten nor attract you. Then you will be able to experience sense pleasures without becoming a slave to them.

In fact, we don't study the Dhamma to shut out the external world or to be enslaved by it, but to arrive at our innate natural freedom. Then we can experience the world as it is, in its beauty and ugliness, in the mundane as well as the extraordinary, without having hang-ups or being caught by life's snares.

Outward Form

D: You said we should neither cling to form nor reject it. How do we know if we are clinging or not?

T: It depends on whether or not you are having conflicts with yourself regarding form. Society requires certain forms. You are expected to behave in a certain way, dress in a certain manner. This conventional truth is called *paññati*. It means knowing which form is appropriate for that situation. But if you cling to the form, your mind will be rigid and you will enslave yourself to form. On the other hand, if you reject the form while you are in it, then you are also enslaved.

D: Why is that so?

When you reject something, you are clinging to your rejection. Your mind becomes fixed on the rejection. Clinging or rejecting, either way, your mind is fixed and can never be free of conflict. You perpetually struggle.

D: How does we get out of this fixation?

You have to transcend the dualism of form as well as of not-form.

You cling to form or reject it because you have set up likes and dislikes in your mind. Perhaps you reject a conventional truth. Although this truth is relative, it is still the established norm for the moment. When you rebel against a form, you are unable to accept things as they are.

D: But how can we accept a form if it is against our better judgment?

That is exactly the point. It is precisely because of our value judgments that we are unable to see things as they are. We see things according to our way of thinking. Our likes and dislikes become our frame of reference. We reject outright anything that does not fit into this framework. Conversely, if something fits into our framework, we embrace it

102

as our possession. Our mind always flits between these two extremes, clinging and rejecting. As long as our minds are polarized in this manner, we continue to be attached. When we are so attached to our likes and dislikes, how can our minds be free to see form as it is?

D: Then what do we do?

There is nothing to do but learn to be silent, to not judge the form. As soon as you stop judging, your likes and dislikes will also cease, as will your clinging and rejecting. Once you stop being judgmental, you will see the form as the form, no more, no less. You will see it as it is and you will be able to relate to it freely.

Unhindered by rejecting or clinging, you can function within form or no-form.

ORDINARY AWARENESS

BEING A CLOSE FRIEND, and closer still in spirit, makes possible open and free communication without constraint either way.

E: *I am aware of a stillness in me that is so peaceful and exquisite that I feel as if I were living in a cocoon.*

T: This is only a phase. It will pass away, and later it will become ordinary. There is nothing extraordinary about peace.

E: *But this is not ordinary! I felt this peace when I was very young, but when I grew up I became filled with emotions, conflicts and frustrations, and I lost this stillness. Only now, through meditation and study of the Dhamma, am I beginning to experience this again! This is a marvelous thing and it is definitely not ordinary. What I mean by ordinary is the angers and frustrations I went through before. I don't have them now. That is what I mean by not being ordinary.*

It is true that the feeling of marvel and exquisiteness makes one think one is enveloped in a cocoon. This is only in the beginning. This feeling of exquisiteness – or whatever you want to call it – will fade away like everything else. For the moment, you feel separate from others and may even think yourself above them. Actually, there is neither above nor below. We are all the same as human beings. We all possess this inner stillness, everyone of us.

We are neither better nor worse than others.

It is just that we are more fortunate than some others because we have been presented with a set of circumstances in which we can learn to experience this inherent inner quality.

E: *You mean everyone has it in them?*

Of course. Most people are not aware of this peace be-

cause they are caught up with their emotions and everything that goes on outside of themselves. In Buddhism, this
is called *moha*, or delusion. Just because we know how to
look within doesn't make us any different from others. If we
think we are different, we are creating a huge gulf between
ourselves and others. We are creating a mental division and
will never be at one with them.

E: But why do you say this awareness of peace is ordinary?

Well, you see, it may seem extraordinary to you now
because for a long time you have been functioning with a
roller-coaster mind. But the newness will wear out and this
awareness of peace will become second nature. Once you
become accustomed to this relatively new state of mind, it
becomes just an ordinary way of being, an everyday awareness. The only difference is that previously your awareness
was tied to the outside world and to your emotions and confusions. Now it has learned to stay in its own peace.

E: But how did we lose our peace?

We never lost peace; it has always been there. We were
just too preoccupied with our emotions and were not aware
of our peaceful state. This peaceful state is nothing extraordinary. But one has to be very careful here. As long as we
think this stillness is extraordinary, we cling to it. This clinging is so subtle and refined that it is difficult to recognize in
oneself. One does not realize that one is still on a very refined ego trip. So long as that is the case, even when one experiences stillness through *samadhi* (concentration), there is
no chance for *pañña* (wisdom) to arise.

E: Why is that?

Even a very concentrated mind, if it is not completely
free, impedes the unfolding of wisdom. You see, in achieving *samadhi*, although you can suppress defilements to some
extent, they are not totally extinguished. *Samadhi* enables the

mind to achieve a sharpness and sensitivity that is greater than ordinary. This sensitivity is what experiences peace and stillness so clearly. Sensitivity has its drawbacks in that the stillness is so unique and exquisite that one clings to its uniqueness. Thus self-importance arises. Many are stuck in this way and are unable to proceed from there.

E: *Don't you need* samadhi *to achieve* pañña *(wisdom)?*

Sure – but let's be clear. There are two kinds of *samadhi*. In addition to *jhanic samadhi*, there is also what is called *khanika samadhi*. It is only momentary in nature but it is penetrating enough to realize Truth. *Khanika samadhi* can occur even without strenuous meditative efforts, given the right circumstances and mental state. Even in *jhanic samadhi*, realization of Truth or *anatta* (not-self) is only momentary. After that, one is back to ordinary consciousness. The unfolding of insight wisdom with *khanika samadhi* occurs with few or none of the mystic experiences or sensations of bliss that are usually encountered in *jhanic samadhi*; thus, the person has no chance to cling to blissful sensations. Before they know it, they are back to ordinary consciousness.

E: *But don't people who experience* khanika samadhi *also accumulate some experiences they hang on to?*

Of course they do, and that is why in all cases there should be a guiding hand to help people free themselves from their own achievements. As I said just now, clinging to progress on the spiritual path is so subtle that it is never easy for us to realize this in ourselves.

E: *Would a teacher know it?*

It depends upon the sensitivity of the teacher and his or her own experience. But a truly wise teacher should be able to detect where the clinging or the problem is and help accordingly. I still remember clearly eighteen years ago when my teachers chastized me mercilessly for getting a swelled head. Thinking back now, I realize how fortunate I was to experience my teachers' great compassion.

E: Wasn't it painful for you at that time?

Of course it was. I was only thirty-three then and the only woman in the Dhamma circle. You can imagine how inflated I became with all the praise and attention I was getting. My teachers saw all of this and took it upon themselves to put me in my right place. They taught me the essence and virtue of humility. From them I learned that spiritual achievement without wisdom and humility is useless to oneself or humanity.

**The essence of the spiritual path lies only in
the beauty of the ordinariness, in the mundane,
and in the freedom from separation of the
spiritual and the ordinary.**

ELABORATION OF
THE NOBLE EIGHTFOLD PATH

1. RIGHT UNDERSTANDING *(samma ditthi)*

Knowledge of the Four Noble Truths:
  a) the Noble Truth of Suffering;
  b) the Noble Truth of Cause of Suffering;
  c) the Noble Truth of the Cessation of Suffering;
  d) the Noble Truth of the Way Leading to the Cessation of Suffering.

2. RIGHT THOUGHTS *(samma sankappa)*

Thoughts free from:
  a) lust, free from attachment;
  b) free from ill-will; and
  c) free from cruelty.

3. RIGHT SPEECH *(samma vaca)*

Refrain from:
  a) falsehood;
  b) slander;
  c) harsh words; and
  d) frivolous speech.

4. RIGHT ACTION *(samma kammanta)*

Abstain from:
  a) killing;
  b) stealing; and
  c) sexual misconduct.

5. RIGHT LIVELIHOOD *(samma ajiva)*

Abstain from trading in:
  a) arms;
  b) human beings (slavery, prostitution, etc.);
  c) flesh (breeding animals for slaughter);
  d) intoxicants; and
  e) poison.

6. RIGHT EFFORT *(samma vayama)*

a) to discard evil that has already arisen;
b) to prevent the arising of unarisen evil;
c) to develop unarisen good; and
d) to promote the good that has already arisen.

7. RIGHT MINDFULNESS *(samma sati)*

Mindfulness with regard to:
a) body;
b) feelings;
c) mental formations; and
d) ideas, thoughts, conceptions and things *(dhammas)*.

8. RIGHT CONCENTRATION *(samma samadhi)*

One-pointedness of mind.

GLOSSARY OF PALI TERMS

Anapanasati: mindfulness of breathing; a form of meditation

Anicca: impermanence, flux, change

Avijja: ignorance of the Four Noble Truths

Brahma vihara: sublime dwelling in universal love, compassion, sympathetic joy and equanimity

Bojjhanga: seven factors of enlightenment, of which mindfulness is the first

Citta-nupassana: contemplation of the mind

Dhamma: truth, teaching, righteousness, doctrine, nature, all things and states, conditioned and unconditioned

Dhamma-nupassana: contemplation on mental/intellectual objects

Dukkha: suffering, conflict, unsatisfactoriness

Jhanic samadhi: trance state in which the mind is absorbed in one mental object

Karuna: compassion

Kaya-nupassana: contemplation of the body

Khanika samadhi: split-second collectedness of the mind

Magga: path or way

Maya: illusions

Metta: universal love

Moha: ignorance

Mudita: sympathetic joy

Nibbana: Ultimate Reality, Absolute Truth, The Unconditioned

Nirodha: cessation of dukkha

Pañña: insight, wisdom

Samadhi: concentration attained in higher meditation

Samatha: concentration meditation

Samma kammanta: right action

Samudaya: arising, origin of dukkha

Satipatthana: setting up of mindfulness

Tadanga nirodha: momentary cessation of suffering

Theravada: literally, "the School of Elders," the orthodox, original form of Buddhism followed in Sri Lanka, Burma, Thailand, Laos and Cambodia

Upekkha: equanimity

Vipassana: insight meditation

Dr. Thynn Thynn is a medical doctor-turned-artist from Burma and a Dhamma teacher. She is the mother of two and currently lives in Sebastopal, CA. She published a book in Burmese in 1978 about her experiences in Buddhist meditation. She is the author of many articles on Buddhism, childhood education and health related issues, published in Thailand and Burma.

For further information, the author can be reached at the following address:

Dr. Thynn Thynn
352 Pleasant Hill Ave. N.
Sebastopal, CA 95472

Living Meditation, Living Insight
The Path of Mindfulness
in Daily Life

For Western practitioners of Buddhist insight, the
application of mindfulness in daily life, rather than
abstract theory, is what connects them most to the
teachings. This book speaks most eloquently on
how the path of mindfulness may be available to
householders with full responsibilities of jobs and
families. The most precious commodity in our busy
daily life is time, and the complexities of life are so
demanding that to find a sense of balance and
sanity seems to be a pressing issue. Dr. Thynn's
focus is on gaining spiritual insight through
keeping mindfulness alive in the midst of our busy
daily lives. Her book is a unique presentation of
traditional Theravada teachings for lay people, and
shows a strong flavor
of Zen and Krishnamurti.

Dr. Thynn Thynn is a medical doctor-turned-artist
from Burma and a Dhamma teacher. She is the
mother of two and currently lives in Scarsdale,
New York. She published a book in Burmese
in 1978 about her experiences in Buddhist
meditation. She is the author of many articles on
Buddhism, childhood education and health related
issues, published in Thailand and Burma.

Dedication of Merit for All Donors

May all the merit and grace gained from adorning Buddha's Pure Land, from loving our parents, from serving our country and from respecting all sentient belngs be transformed and transferred for the benefit and salvation of all suffering sentient beings on the three evil paths. Furthermore, may we who read and hear this Buddhadharma, and thereafter, generate our Bodhi Minds be reborn, at end of our lives, in the Pure Land.

Living Meditation Living Insight

Reprinted and donated for free distribution by

The Buddhist Association of Canada

Cham Shan Temple

7254 Bayview Avenue, Thornhill, Ontario, Canada L3T 2R6

Tel : 905-886-1522

www.chamshantemple.org

承 印 處：福峰圖書光碟有限公司

地　　址：台北市士林區永公路500巷48號

Tel:886-2-2862-0707 Fax:886-2-2861-7023

E-mail:fufong.fufong@msa.hinet.net

歡迎翻印・功德無量

2011年2月　　恭印2000冊

FL-4288